THE BIG ISSUE BOOK

EDITED BY MARTIN DUNKERTON AND SKY

From a sheltered

flame

SIMON & SCHUSTER

LONDON·SYDNEY·NEW YORK·TOKYO·SINGAPORE·TORONTO

Acknowledgements

Our first big thanks is to the sponsors and everyone involved directly or indirectly with *The Big Issue Book;* that is to all those in the book, and also to those who were inspirational in making *From A Sheltered Flame* happen.

The sponsors: Adrian Ensor Ltd (black and white printing); Artworkers (design); Ilford Photographic Company Ltd (paper and materials); Silver Foundry (equipment); Your Business Partner Ltd (accountancy).

The organisations, groups, centres and charities throughout Britain who helped make this book: The Photographers' Gallery; St Martin-in-the-Fields Social Care Unit (London); Cardiff City Centre Youth Project; The Grass Market Project (Edinburgh); London Connection; New Horizon (London); West London Day Centre; North Lambeth Day Centre; St Botolphs (London); Portugal Prints (London); the MARK Project (Liverpool); Liverpool City Council Housing Dept; Hereford and Worcestershire Social Services Dept; Lambeth Social Services Dept; NACRO; Shelter; NCH; NAYPIC; SHAC; CHAR; West London Mission; Centrepoint; and the Bayswater Hotel Homelessness Project.

The individuals who have been supportive generally or specifically: Martin Fletcher; Daphne Bien; Adrian Ensor; Eve Barker; Steve Wallace; Lucie Russell; Tiffany Andersen; Julie Swallow; Constable Wallard; The Dunkerton family; Carol Barker; Sam Hutton; Kia Miller; Clare Kafourous; Sam Heath; SJ; Chris Birkett; Peter Horrocks; RN Commander Robert Green (retired); Richard and Andy Johnson; Gunn Brinson; the John family; Rikki Shields; Rising Buffalo; Edi Wolley; the Newman family; John Davie; Jill Neville; Charles Milne; Dick Ross; Derek Wallbank; Yvette Vanson; Michael Mansfield QC; Tristan and Dennis Anthony; Sue New; Stevie Bezencenet; Jason James; Mark Risso-Gill; Richard Kravetz; Terence Wilton; Ishia Bennison; Tex.

Also, our gratitude to the many others who have helped along the way, but who are not listed here.

Martin Dunkerton and *The Big Issue.*
September 1993

SPONSORS
Ilford Photographic Company Ltd
Adrian Ensor Ltd
Silver Foundry
Artworkers
Your Business Partner Ltd

Contents

A note to readers

The big issue of homelessness is that its root causes lie hidden in everyday life and can literally affect anyone - from a millionaire to a coal miner.

From A Sheltered Flame explores that unnecessary experience powerfully, in images, words and poetry; and its commitment to positive change is uniquely shown by homeless people being involved in the making of the book.

To us, the Flame represents the soul. We sincerely hope the book touches yours.

After school skipping, Cheatham Hill, Manchester, 1985.

Foreword by Anita Roddick

There is no way we wouldn't have supported *The Big Issue*. We've always maintained that a leg up is better than a hand out. Give people the chance to help themselves, and everyone is happier in the long run. The inspiring thing about *The Big Issue* is that it hasn't taken a long run - the paper has got off to a flying start and hasn't stopped since. It's become a dynamic and desperately needed new voice, not just because it provides a forum to people who previously had none, but also because it offers opportunities for new talents to explore their creative abilities. The fruits of those abilities are contained in this book. They are more than a tribute to *The Big Issue*'s relevance. By illuminating and humanising the statistics of homelessness, they underscore just how deep and shaming the problem is. The shame is ours. May the solution also rest with us and those we entrust to make positive changes on our behalf.
The Big Issue is a start.

Spitalfields, 1981.

Spitalfields, 1983.

Introduction by John Bird

editor of The Big Issue

The Big Issue, a paper sold by the homeless, is not a new idea. Since the 1980s, *Street News* has been sold on the streets of New York by the homeless and the jobless. Gordon Roddick, chairman of the Body Shop brought the idea back to London and it eventually saw the light of day in the summer of 1991. Our original intention was to give homeless people the opportunity to earn a living other than by begging.

It was very simple therefore in its initial approach. It never set out to change the social fabric of Britain. It was modest. Sold on the streets, the vendor would get the lion's share of the cover price. There were no tricks. Money went directly into the homeless people's pockets rather than being thrown to a third party to dole it out later.

Our first problem in *The Big Issue* was that unless the public wanted to buy the paper, then it wasn't a legitimate deal. If they were buying it as a pity purchase, then it was just a hidden hand-out. It couldn't simply be about homelessness because you could not build a large enough readership, and no large readership meant no income for the homeless. *The Big Issue* had to be something that homeless people wanted to sell and the public wanted to buy. We expanded the arts pages, put in personality interviews and tried to make it work as a good read as well as a social read.

We gave homeless people an opportunity to earn their own living and to stand on their own two feet; it was about empowering people and giving them an alternative to dependency culture.

When *The Big Issue* first started, no one knew the importance of the contribution that homeless writers would make to the paper. When we went out and tried to get homeless people to write for us, it was as a means of giving variety to our pages. We felt that the more the homeless were involved, the more the paper could claim that it was giving them a chance to stand on their own two feet. We soon began to realize that we had to offer them more than pages and income. The 'Capital Lights' writing group developed out of an increasing awareness that we were missing a wasted opportunity. That people didn't need ideal conditions to work, but encouragement, paper and a large table.

Hostels, doorways, night shelters and squats are not the best places to take up the art of writing. How many times have you heard of aspirant writers saying that until they get the ideal conditions in which to write they are incapable of writing? Excuses abound: to write you need peace and tranquillity, a computer and the encouragement of others.

Alas, the world is not so perfect. And some of the best writing is carried out in the most appalling conditions, often by the people you least expect. This collection of work exposes the lie that until you've moved into a Habitat catalogue, have an encouraging array of encouragers, along with the right programmed Amstrad, you can't achieve anything.

Why? Because From A Sheltered Flame is not simply about writing. It's about living on the edge of things. It's about surviving and making sense of the wobblies thrown at you by circumstance. It's about creating and making it, whilst living in hell and still seeing purpose in who you are and what you are. It's about experience.

To talk about homeless people simply as people without a roof is to ignore the complexity and the centrality of homelessness. Homelessness is the result of a massive social failure originating in the late Sixties: not to see this is to trivialize it. And one has only to talk to a handful of homeless people to realize it.

From A Sheltered Flame in its writing, poetry, and photographs attempts to show points of view which go beyond our normal perceptions. It digs into the root causes of being faced with no home.

In our social fabric, housing, education, health, industry, and local government are all interwoven. Close a colliery in Nottingham and a young person from there could end up homeless in the Strand, London. That unfortunately, is quite simply how homelessness works. The collapse of our manufacturing industrial base and the ending of benefits for sixteen and seventeen-year-olds in the 1980s hasn't helped. The demise of service industries and the white-collar sector in the 1990s just reinforced the idea that no one could

escape the prospect of job losses, house repossessions, or ending up homeless: and certainly the break-up of families is evidence of increasing social problems which unless addressed will be the cause of a whole new generation of dispossessed children with no visible means of support.

The photographs by Martin Dunkerton prominently feature children: the images poignantly reveal the social connections and central causes of the homelessness condition. His images also go further, and startlingly reveal not only the tragic effects on people's lives, but also what is being done to resolve the issue. For many photographers it is easier to take images of homeless people by stepping back: not getting their hands dirty. Depicting the homeless as passive or as interesting objects of photographic art, to be hung in galleries without context or understanding is an insult to us all, not just the homeless. Martin's photographs delve deep within the homeless psyche, they penetrate through the outer core and into the inner meanings. They break stereotypes, whilst suggesting ways forward. This positive approach is what The Big Issue is about.

The writing by Sky and Allan Meaken, has developed from The Big Issue's writing workshops and is a progression from their published work in the magazine. They, like many other writers, have developed skills they would never have believed possible years before. Their skills in interviewing techniques have been essential to draw a truth from the lives of the eight poets. Their straightforward approach has been to allow each poet's voice to be heard, rather than having their stories told for them. How much of history is told like this? Sky and Allan have not only been homeless themselves, but know many of the homeless people they are interviewing personally. This, I believe, shows in their being able to achieve write-ups that are challenging, moving and direct.

The poetry has been written from the streets, bed and breakfasts, squats and hostels. The poems tell the tales of people's agonies, histories and hopes. The quality of much of the work is unsurpassed. There is no excuse. The poems stand on their own two feet. Each poem is a testament to the author's resilience in the face of pain and suffering that many of us can only guess at. The section of anonymous poetry holds a message for us all: that to bypass an individual is to ignore their potential, talent, or even brilliance.

The design has been assisted by John Gregg, a current vendor, who has topped up old training and work skills with Eve Barker of Artworkers, the design company which has sponsored him to help create the vibrant look of the book. John has learnt state of the art design techniques and production, which have been essential to make the book something people see and want to buy: a principle the magazine has applied with success.

Martin Dunkerton enabled Sandra Clifford, poet and ex-vendor, with the technical skills to use a medium format camera, so she could take the photographic portraits. Her approach in the image making reveals a tenderness and directness, showing the talent of someone who knows her subjects. This approach is basic to getting a book project like this right.

In editing the book, Martin and Sky wielded a strong collaboration of skill, knowledge and understanding as well as a sheer perseverance to make it all happen. *From A Sheltered Flame*'s evolution as a whole has been fraught with the usual problems associated with putting together something of worth. Martin Dunkerton came in out of the blue with the book idea one day in early 1992, and it has taken the best part of a year for him to work with *Big Issue* ex- and current homeless vendors, to produce a book which reflects the aims and aspirations of the magazine.

The Big Issue was founded on Anita Roddick's Trade not Aid philosophy, the principles of which have been applied to this book. Martin Fletcher, the commissioning editor at Simon and Schuster, took the project on with the same principle: the publisher makes profit out of *The Big Issue*'s name, and so do we, in receiving royalties

from each copy sold. One major difference in Martin's approach which set him apart from other publishers was his willingness to take on the enabling aspect of the magazine into the book's production.

The integration of talents of the company sponsors, the two Martins and our vendors set a system of working which all sides learnt and developed, coming together to produce a book of excellence. The book therefore, must be seen as a unique document that highlights both that commitment and that determination.

If you manage to get from these pages a sense of this strength and, at the same time, grasp the essence of the voice of the streets, then hopefully you will be drawn into standing up and fighting to end the gross social iniquity of homelessness.

If nothing else, *From A Sheltered Flame* needs to be read for its inventiveness and imagination. We hope you have a good read.

Contributors

School children, Rhymney Valley, 1985.

*Martin Dunkerton,
photographer, book co-ordinator,
co-editor*

Martin was born in 1963 and is a BA graduate (LCP) and MA (Royal College of Art) trained stills photographer and film writer/director. He has directed for both Channel 4 and BBC, and won a gold award for his RCA drama *Fire and Steel* in the Chicago Film Festival. He was nominated for a Royal Television Society Award for his BBC documentary *Black Diamonds*, which followed his first book *Is it still raining in Aberfan?* In early 1992, Martin found himself unemployed. He used the time to finish writing two long-standing feature screenplays; 'Secret Crossing' and 'The Great Awakening', and originated *The Big Issue Book* after several inspiring meetings with poets, including the homeless poet and writer Sky. Martin reflected on his own brief time of homelessness, when he was a student, which led him to research poetry from thoughout the country and use his lifetime's photographic work to create *From A Sheltered Flame*.

Sky,
writer, poet, co-editor

Sky was born in 1967 and brought up in Reading. After naval college, Sky worked in London as a courier, but found himself homeless. For two years, he battled against the effects of living on the streets. After two suicide attempts, Sky found sanctuary and direction putting together (with a Prince's Trust Grant) a booklet of poetry called 'An Act of Silence'. The booklet was made up of poetry by him and other homeless people and proved extremely successful, selling out within months. In 1991, Sky met the editor of *The Big Issue*, John Bird, and was brought in as one of the first vendors and writers for the magazine. In 1992, Sky won a hard earned bid for a council flat and a place at university studying for a degree in social policy, where he is at present. Sky's intention is to work within the European Community, specifically Eastern Europe, in respect of housing and economic policy. Sky became involved in *The Big Issue Book* after meeting Martin in 1992, and worked in between studies to complete the writing and co-editing of the project in 1993.

Allan Meaken,
writer

Allan was born in 1936 and moved from his native Australia to England fifteen years ago. Allan went into the Merchant Navy, then in the hotel trade, but became homeless in 1992 after he fell ill and lost his job. Allan began selling *The Big Issue* and attended the writing groups, where he wrote features not only for the magazine, but for the *New Statesman* and art journals. Allan is still homeless in a hostel and hopes to find real accommodation soon. His immediate plans are to complete a course in word processing, then to go on to a course in journalism at City University. Allan's long-term aim is to complete a novel and to continue writing as a freelance journalist for national magazines and newspapers. Allan's involvement in *From A Sheltered Flame* is due to his commitment to writing, and support for *The Big Issue* magazine.

Sandra Clifford,
poet, portrait photographer

Sandra was born in 1975 and brought up in London. After being sexually abused at home, Sandra moved between care and home, but eventually left for London's West End with a friend. They lived rough, sleeping on the streets and in hostels. Sandra stopped begging when she was introduced, via a vendor, to *The Big Issue*. She began selling the magazine herself and after several months was offered a full time job working in distribution. Sandra regularly attended *The Big Issue* writing workshops and, as her poetry began to be published, she started taking photographs for the 'Capital Lights' section of the magazine. Sandra has since found accommodation and has won a place on a secretarial course, after which she intends to follow a career as a company PA. Sandra became involved in *The Big Issue Book* because she wanted her story to be told, and saw her poetry and photography as a continuation and development of her work for the magazine.

John Gregg,
assistant designer

John was born in 1963 and was brought up near Harrow. John went to private school and later Watford College, where he obtained a printing diploma. John found work in the printing industry, but was laid off in June 1992, as a direct result of the recession. He had to sell his car and in spite of promises from his boss, didn't receive any redundancy money. The final straw was when John broke up with his girlfriend and was illegally evicted from his rented flat when he got behind with his payments. John ended up sleeping rough in the Strand and Rickmansworth, then fortunately discovered *The Big Issue* and became a vendor. John has since moved into a bed and breakfast and has become a 'vendor of the fortnight'. He has appeared on Channel 4's 'Parliament' and been interviewed for the BBC's 'World Service' news programme. John hopes to move out of his b & b soon and find permanent accommodation. He became involved in *The Big Issue Book* to learn modern printing technology and design, which he is certain will help him find work in the future.

Porthcawl, the traditional miners' holiday destination, 1990.

Poetry, images, words...

Alison Traille

Alison was born in 1974. She is better known as Ali to her friends, and was sixteen when she was thrown out of her home. Family conflict can often be healed, but like any fracture in a young person's emotional life it can take time before the pain can go. For some, it never leaves, only remains hidden. For Ali, talking and writing about her experiences has been a first step to exposing the hurt and letting it go.

'I came from a middle-class family, my ancestors were Irish aristocrats. I never thought I would end up being homeless. My life was in ruins when I first got thrown out of home. I tried to seek help from the police and Department of Social Security. I slept from friend to friend, from sleeping bag to couch, whatever I could find or was given.

'All my life I have been moved around, switching and changing from one relation to another. From private school, to comprehensive. It's been really hard because I was always at the top of the class for all of my subjects. Busting up with my stepfather and mother then leaving home was incredibly frightening and I wondered whether it was to be the beginning part of a downward spiral.'

After sleeping rough for several months and in several squats, Alison finally got into bed and breakfast accommodation. 'I tried to claim money from the DSS, but failed, which reduced me to tears. I suddenly realized how many people were in the same situation as me and was really upset that so many people were treated that way. I had always written poetry,

but suddenly I wrote poems that reflected where I was. Homeless.'

Whilst in the b & b Alison bought a copy of *The Big Issue* and realized she was eligible to sell the paper. After several weeks of selling, Alison decided to send one of her poems to the 'Capital Lights' section. 'I didn't think they would print my poem. When I saw it published, I was really surprised and elated. Looking back I think it's extremely important that our writing is shown. The 'Capital Lights' section achieves that, and gave me real hope.

'I went to one of *The Big Issue* writing workshops and met similar people to myself, but of all ages. That was an experience. It was a melting pot of ideas, everyone brought something new to it each week. It not only helped me develop my poetry, but gave me the strength of will to get out of my b & b and into a hostel, which I must confess is only marginally better.'

At the writing workshop Alison developed a specific philosophy of what it is like being homeless. 'Being without a home is like being on a ship chartered by someone else, with someone else navigating. It's very difficult to be in control. It's hard enough to survive. Everyone you meet from the streets is going through a personal turmoil. We all have left something behind, like belongings we may run into again to collect, if they're not too damaged, lost, or stolen.'

Alison's poems are significantly multi-layered and reflect a very strong spiritual sense which she finds difficult, but also challenging to deal with. I suppose I just know it's there. I sense things, deep things about people around me. It's as though people have an aura about them which I pick up. It can be negative or positive, but is also affected by how I feel. I believe we all have a sixth sense, we just have to learn how

to use it again, it's something latent which is gradually being re-learnt. The good in people will naturally come out and things will change for the better.'

Alison describes the journey to where she is now as only part of the way. 'I have so much more to learn. My confidence suddenly slips, then rises again. It's like a yo-yo. Sometimes I think about how I got here and how easy it is to not actually move on a rung of the ladder. It's so important to believe in yourself and have someone believe in you, otherwise you can just slip back down.'

Alison remembers life on the streets and in hostels. 'The people I met were people I'd never have met in a million years if I hadn't been homeless. I was middle class and they thought I was pretending, they called me 'plastic homeless'. But I was homeless, I was in exactly the same situation as them. I had come from my home which was broken, like most of them. My family didn't want me and the homeless community didn't want me either, I felt outcast.'

Alison had to tread carefully but gradually made some important friends amongst the homeless community. 'Lots of them loved me because I am different and quirky, we used to argue about politics and laugh at observations about homelessness. I felt many of my friends' deep pain which they kept inside, and I respected their ability to survive.'

Alison's own ability to survive has been her chameleon-like approach to her surroundings. After searching for a specific direction with her writing, Alison decided that acting was what she really wanted to pursue. 'I always wanted to be an actress. I was in the Young Vic theatre when I was fourteen and loved it, I was passionate about it and I felt a huge urge to work and be with other actors.

'When you are actually up there on stage the feelings you have are so amazing. You feel wanted, needed and strong. When you know you have something positive to give to others it spurs you on. I love the emotion, the passion and power of the performance.

'I have had the strength to make contact with my mother and we have broken down the barriers and are actually talking much more on a one-to-one basis, rather than just mother-daughter, which is why we argued so much before.

'I hope to move out of the hostel soon and move into a bedsit. It will be a new start for me which will stabilize my acting career. I have just won a part in a play called 'Under the Carpet' which is about schizophrenia and deals with government policy on psychiatric institutions. It's strange, being homeless was like rehearsing, not for acting, but for life. Finally, I'm ready.'

A SPECIAL FRIEND

You can't use people and abuse them,
How can you strip a soul,
Like ripping the bark from a tree.

Roots gnarled and twisted up in the heart,
Planted steadfastly.

Lies, lies. Everything we are told.
Drummed into us time and time again.
Why didn't you accept it?

Who did you think you were fooling,
I watched it bite into your flesh,
Sank its sharpened teeth in
And drew blood. Your precious blood.
Spilt chops in the dust,
You thought I deceived you.

Animals ripped you up.
They left you for dead.
I wish I could have seen it in your eyes,
To get your view.

Oh, a tangled web your body entwined,
Waiting to be captured and killed.
But I never was.

You travelled while living on a string,
But it wasn't just a string.
A taut piece of elastic,
Which pushed you to the edge,
And brought you back,
Back to nothing.

Memories are always happy,
Unless they are sad,
And although I cannot yet
Fully understand your death

I will continue to fight,
Not for a lost cause,

But to beat this hunter,
Killing us helpless newborn men.

Alison Traille
Dedicated to the memory of Stuart Duckworth.
Born 1967 - died 1992. Sadly missed.

Miners, Taff Merthyr Colliery, Treharris, 1990.

Going clubbing, Notting Hill Gate, London, 1992.

EXTRACT FROM
'ANY NIGHT WITH YOU'

Bed is possessed
By some form,
I think it is love.

But with me it is lost,
In the soft folds and dunes
Of your hands.

Except the back of your neck
Your curling hair,
I wrap around my finger,
I cannot place my body around it.

Instead I will lay next to you,
And I think how lucky I am,
To be loved by you.

I'd still like to know,
Do you do what I do,
Watching me asleep,
Admiring the wonder of it all.

And lovingly, screaming,
Me, awake, again.

Did I never sit up at night
Holding you, listening to your crying,
Watching your tears.

Holding you to my breast,
Like a child,
Hot tears running rivulets down
To my stomach,
Soothing you, comforting you,
Loving you.

But I never did remember.
You holding me all night while I cried.
You, you held me while I cried,
during the day.

But at night you slept while I cried.
Only the soft moon,
And the horses felt my tears,
Loving you in life and death.

Alison Traille

UNTITLED POEM

Shocked, stunned
I let the night drift and spin
Through the bitter-sweet scent of alcohol.

Drugs, forgetting
Blotting the pain out,
Now there is a void,
No sleep. No food. No love.

I can't accept anything into me again,
I learn by my mistakes,
I am not to blame,
It's in his mind
And constantly on my mind.

Tears bled dry my eyes
Sickness sweeps through my stomach
Concentration is blurry and hazed.

I think I may as well do
Some more drink and drugs,
But I still can't forget.

Alison Traille
19th January 1992

UNTITLED

I am angry
I will crush you under my boot.
My ugly thoughts are under control
After trying to decipher what yours are,
And what they mean.

White linen on a yellow clothes line,
And a peach negligee with green and red pegs,
I will cast iron bricks down on your fragile body.

Crushingly, suffocating with dust,
And earthworms
As a brown spider with speckled legs
I am writing for you
In my beautifully woven web,
While feathers blow from the force,
That is the wind.

And a peg sits distantly in the corner,
Swathed in coral curtains.
I hear a tapping of what my hate will do for me.
It will break me, shatter me, ruin me, hate me,
Then scatter the millions of tiny precious
pieces of fire.

Alison Traille
2nd August 1992

Home-help, Herefordshire, 1985.

Lambeth playgroup, Brixton, 1985.

AMANDA'S ROOM

Trees sparkle in the cold wind,
Car doors reflecting the cloudy moon,
I am willing to be taken there,
Two women, dancing in a scarlet room.

Where broken hearts and spilt tears
Lay scattered like petals on the floor,
I am a moon type, I worship the right planet
I know I am irrevocably tied to my fate.

While doorbells will interrupt me
And make me jump,
I feel so awful,
The people next door would like to go bed.

I will do the same too,
Soon.

Cold, stale chips and alcohol,
Shocked by intolerable behaviour.
I will listen to the fierce wind
rattle in the windows.

Alison Traille
11th January 1993

UNTITLED POEM

I need to be alone,
In my writing I find solace.

Peace within my inner self,
Looking around me, I see conversation.
Unaware of talk,
I observe as a writer, I see.

I wield a pen,
It's my only guard,
You call it a weapon.

But then why would I want to do anybody
Any harm?

Alison Traille
4th February 1992

UNTITLED POEM

Crying for a family
That never was
But I lied.

I'm not crying,
I don't need to,
Why should I cry for
What I've never had.

Alison Traille
26th March 1992

Manchester, 1986.

Family, opposite Ravenscraig Steelworks, Motherwell, Scotland, 1985.

Family, burns unit, Glasgow Royal Infirmary, 1985.

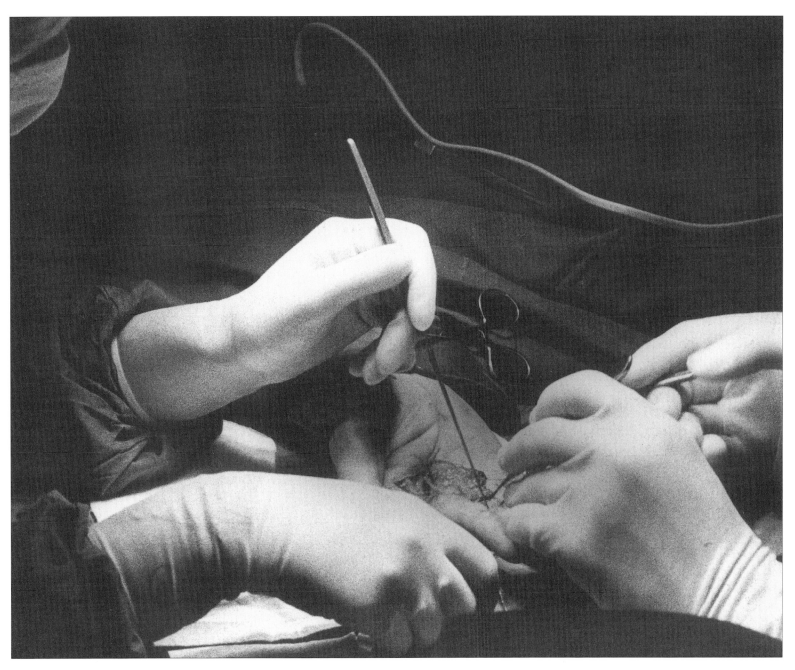

Glasgow Royal Infirmary, 1985.

'Fighting for jobs', South Wales, 1984 - coal vs nuclear power (over 100,000 jobs have been lost in the coal industry since 1984, whilst nuclear power has been subsidised by around £1.2 billion pounds a year since 1989).

Women's strike support group, welfare halls, Upton, Yorkshire, 1985.

Ian Byrne

Ian was born in 1959 in Camberwell, just down the road from where Michael Caine was born and raised. The poet Robert Browning came from there as well. Ian grew up in some old tenements, and after moving to another estate he moved to Peckham before eventually moving to Bromley in Kent. He moved about a lot. After finding himself on the streets, Ian's nomadic existence has only recently stopped.

'When I was eight, me and my brother were put into various foster homes for our own protection. My dad used to beat me up a lot so they had to. two years later Mum and Dad were divorced and we went back to Mum who brought us up. I was totally rebellious by then. I hated everyone and I took it out on everyone. I was so angry with my family but I didn't realize that until I was twenty-four and my brother asked me what I was trying to prove. That always sticks in my mind, that's when I started to grow up.'

Ian talks about the consequences of his parents cruelty. 'If you're one of eight kids and your mum never shows you any love and your dad is always beating you up, you grow up not being able to love because you don't know what love is. Anyway when I was twenty-one I had a fight with my brother and got kicked out. I ended up on the streets of London not trusting anyone and having to be very wary. There are some good people on the streets but it took me a long time to trust anyone. I was streetwise and I suppose that helped me to survive.'

In spite of Ian's experiences, his positive thinking

remains undiminished. 'I like to think that some good will come of this, all that suffering and all that pain can't be for nothing. I'm an optimist, I don't know why but I feel that things will change for me and that good things will happen, and that feeling can never be taken away.

'We were poor when I was growing up. I remember being the only one in the school football team who couldn't afford any boots. There were eight kids to feed and clothe and that can't have been easy for Dad especially with Mum nagging him all the time. We lived on top of each other in a two-bedroomed council flat, it was very difficult for anyone to have any privacy.'

Ian was brought up in the Sixties, and in those days if a man hit his wife the police never got involved. It was called a 'domestic' and it was the same if he hit his children. Ian explains, 'Some kids are good, some kids are bad but I think my dad hit us because he used to drink. He died from drinking but before he died I made my peace with him. I'm so glad I did because I realize now how important it is to be able to forgive.'

Ian went into care and remains bitter about how the system works. 'I don't think putting me into care helped at all. The staff never seemed to understand what was in the children's heads. They put a roof over your head and they fed you but anything else was a rare bonus. If you take a lot of problem children and put them in the same nest, obviously, sparks are going to fly sooner or later and I ended up in an approved school in Essex. I calmed down a bit after that because they threatened me with borstal but I eventually ended there anyway.'

Ian got a job in the building trade when he left the approved school at sixteen, and liked working there. 'I was a good worker. I felt good when I picked up my wage packet, like I had really earned it, but in the building trade you are never guaranteed of work all year round. When the work ran out I became homeless and

subsequently could no longer find gainful employment having no fixed address.

'I slept in squats all over the place and if I couldn't get into a squat I'd sleep on the streets. Some of the places were very dangerous and I was always on tenterhooks, always on my guard. There's good and bad in every society and it's the same in Cardboard City. There's a real sense of kinship amongst the underclasses, a kindred spirit flying in the face of adversity.

'Sooner or later the weather gets really cold and you've got to go inside. I've stayed in all kinds of DHSS hostels and spare houses but I can never settle in them. In one place I can't sleep for the noise and in the next it will be the silence that keeps me awake. There was a lot of people doing drugs as well and I had to tell them to keep away from me but they still kept me awake with their noise. These places are essential for people on the street. They need somewhere to go when they've been heavy on the drink but the government closes them down anyway.

'I wrote my first poem when I was four, it was about a Robin in a tree. I wrote poems for years and years. People said my work was good and that boosted my confidence but after a while I thought, Well it can't be that good, and I'd look in the mirror expecting to see a halo and there wasn't one, just the same person I'd always been.

'I put a lot into my work. Most of my work comes from the heart, there's no falseness in any of it, that's how a good poet should be. I've read all the greats, Byron, Shelley, Keats, Coleridge and Tennyson. You can always tell a great poet because they will move you, it comes from the heart.

'When I write about my experiences it's like letting the ghosts out of their cage. For a while, the ghosts that haunt me disappear and a great

weight is lifted from my shoulders. I am relieved that I can channel it in some way. It makes me a better person.'

After years of having little self-esteem Ian finally feels that he is gaining the self-confidence to make things happen. 'I want to write books, three books and a play. I've got potential, we all have. I'd like to be able to share the experiences of my childhood through my writing so that I can perhaps teach others to love their children who matter, that's how we leave our mark on this Earth.

'If I'm successful in the future I will always fight for the homeless and somewhere along the line I'm going to help children who have been abused in some way. For the moment, though, I help out in the kitchen at St Botolph's making sandwiches and cups of tea for the old dossers and I'm going to a rally at Islington Town Hall to talk about homelessness. I've been on a couple of lobbies to Parliament which at the end of the day didn't really achieve anything; even though there was massive support from the Church, the business sector didn't do what it set out to do.'

Ian's unending approach is set out with a clear philosophy for the future, and a pragmatism for us either to accept, reject, or just contemplate. 'If I could implement change in this world I would like to see everyone with a roof over their heads, food in their stomachs, and proper shoes on their feet. There are so many temptations in life, drinks, drugs, money, you have to be strong to say: I'm not having any today. Money means nothing to me. If I had a million pounds I'd probably give it all away. Don't get me wrong, it's nice to have few bob now and again but I'm really not interested in money. Life would be so much better without money. It would put an end to most crime and everyone would have a chance for a real job. A day is dawning when driving a Rolls-Royce will be like wearing a mink coat!'

Aylesham, Kent, 1985.

Salford, 1986.

Ravenscraig Steelworks, Motherwell, Scotland 1985 (closed 1992).

THE POWER OF MONEY

If you can afford academic qualifications
In a class-structured civilization
People who dominate the world through money
Are out of touch which is very funny.

They see value as a status symbol
That either become rich or crash in a windfall
those that have nothing feel a class pain
Not capable of grammar, but only when they train.

Incredible it sounds in total confusion
Exploding like an atom bomb in fusion
Credit cards made of plastic
That make life easy and very drastic.

So what is the answer to a balanced society
being rich and famous with notoriety
Money is a false image that makes people ruthless
But what of the working class who are penniless.

Those on the dole can't be extravagant
Afford luxurious possessions that are elegant
The most important thing is to live life
Fight for a belief against tyranny and strife.

So why do they spend, spend, spend
When people are at their tether till the end
A structure of monopolies for people who work
Just to own a yacht, a mansion, or a Merc.

Ian Byrne

JOAN CRAWFORD ('MOMMIE DEAREST')

Mommie dearest why do you treat me this way
make me wash and scrub and polish all day
Intoxicated with the thought of germs
Because she's frightened of cockroaches and worms.

Wash the bathroom and clean the sink
Clean the dresser with the colour pink
Oh Mommie dearest you are a star
No need for petty innuendos to go so far.

You have a career, so why do you persecute me
Can't you realize what you are doing, can't you see
Be content that you have all the trappings of success
And control the urge for cleanliness.

Oh Mommie dearest I love you anyway
But don't let me hate you and make you pay
You treat me like a little monster all the time
Won't even let me sing any more nursery rhymes.

Please help me by helping yourself
Not shut me out and swirl in your own wealth
You are a good actress so play the proper part
Not tease me and punish me and break my heart.

Insinuating, accusing me of all kinds of things
Taking jewellery, like the time you said I stole your ring
Oh Mommie dearest, where are my rights
You always go into tantrums, cause arguments and fights.

Ian Byrne

THE HARSHNESS OF A DOSSER

The true perspective of life
Is surreal to reconnoitre
A bleeding affinity of a beggar
Who has the impudence to frown.

A victim of circumstance
With a grievance against society
Can't help but recognize
those afflictions to themselves.

An idler who sleeps rough
With an added sense of danger
that creeps around the corner
Lurks where no-one can see.

The strength of their character
Is a portrayal of loyalty
their ordeal is hard enough
but do people really understand.

The police make it a vendetta
Penetrating the undesirables
Who know the fury of their power
Banged away to be forgotten.

Why are people so vindictive
Must be because they're wanderers.
Nomads of the streets of London
Will we ever see any change?

Ian Byrne

Near Gartcosh Steelworks, Scotland, 1985 (closed 1986).

Stockwell, Lambeth, London, 1985.

Unemployed man, Elephant and Castle, London, 1984.

Salford, 1986.

Post riots, Brixton, Lambeth, 1985.

THE IGLOO MAN

He is called the Igloo Man
Wanders the streets of London
In a trance to all around
Seems possessed with a silence.

Been here some fifteen years
Keeps putting on clothing
To hide from himself from the world
A shell to hide from the cold.

Never takes off clothing to wash
With a long black beard
Hair full of lice
Clothing stuck to his body.

Never sits down any more
For fear of breaking his back
Clothes stiff and worn away
His body is totally concealed.

You see his hands sometimes
When he has a cup of tea
The Igloo Man is an alien
Locked inside his own mind.
The fleas jump all over him
People avoid his presence
Step out of his way
Make him feel so low.

Ian Byrne

ME

Mama why don't you show me any affection
Place your love in the right direction
Stop Papa from beating me all the time
Divorce the bastard and everything will be fine.

Always drunk and drooling and slurring
Causing unnecessary hardship, berserking,
Hitting my Mama and causes cuts and bruises
But in the end he is the only one who loses.

Putting me in hospital because he was so cruel
Vindictive, sadistic with no scruples as a rule
Mama placing me in care to protect me
Destroying what love was left in our family tree.

Alone but with a big family to feed
And getting caught for the callousness of his deed
Missing my family going to foster homes
Trying to escape in a wondrous roam.

Growing up with a grudge against them all
By hurting my dignity and making me look small
From children's homes to approved schools
being rebellious and breaking the rules.

From school to prison in a transition
An outcast of society without position.

Out of work, stealing to stay alive
Getting into drugs and moody old dives
From early age to a grown-up man
With an inferior complex no one understands.

Ian Byrne

Television image of riots, Brixton, Lambeth, 1985.

Students rally against cut-backs in grants and further education, London, 1986.

House building has been reduced in Britain by 72 per cent since 1979.

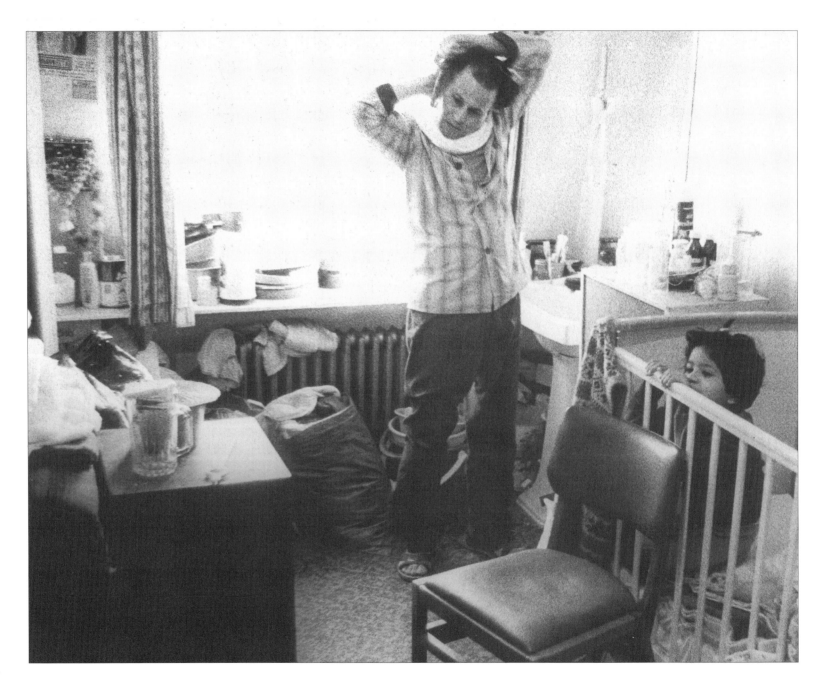

Homeless family with child of four years, bed and breakfast hotel, Bayswater, 1986 - cost to the taxpayer, £15,000 in first year.

Aberfan, 1991.

Homeless man, Portobello Road, London, 1982.

Sandra Clifford

Sandra was born in 1975. She has an immensely strong inner self, which her soft, gentle appearance belies. Sandra's determination and enthusiasm comes from surviving her past and laying to rest some of the ghosts that occasionally still come to haunt her. Sandra has spent many of her eighteen years battling against the sexual and physical abuse that many children have suffered but few are able to express in words. Sandra's poetry remains a testament to the thousands of unheard voices. And perhaps, unknowingly or knowingly, is an open letter to her mother.

'We weren't rich, we weren't poor. I was brought up by my mum, in what seemed a big house, but I never knew my father, and I still haven't met him. My mum was an alcoholic and was going out with someone who was my stepdad at the time, who helped bring me up. I didn't get on with him at all. He didn't treat me like a human being. He treated me worse than an animal. I only started writing poems last year. I can't remember things until I end up having dreams about them. If I was to think now about my past I wouldn't remember anything, except what is in the poems.'

Sandra's poetry graphically exposes her predicament, but her problems began when she was not old enough to express a view or feelings. 'I wanted to tell my mother lots of times about the abuse, but I was scared of what she would think and scared of what she might do. I thought she would think it was my fault, or that I was leading him on. So I never told her. If

I ever did try to say anything, he used to be always there. He would say that I was making things up or that I was a little baby and that's what children do, just to get attention.

'I have told my current boyfriend, Paul, who is very understanding. When we go together and visit my mum's new husband, he and Paul would get a bit drunk and Paul would tell him about what happened to me when I was smaller. I just see my mum's face in my mind and I end up denying everything. I'm afraid that my mum would disown me, more than she has already.

'It's still all confusing to me. I end up looking back in my dreams, and can't go to sleep at night. Paul is the only person who I have really told. He settles me down and tells me not to worry about it and that no one is going to hurt me any more.'

Sandra's education suffered as a result of her abuse, with lack of concentration and getting into trouble with her peers. 'I first went into care when I was sixteen because my mum was beating me up and no one took any notice until I showed them the bruises on my body. So they put me in a hotel for a while and then eventually sent me to a children's home and then an independent unit. I went back to my mum's when it closed for decorations. My mum's drink problem affected me badly because she had no one else to take it out on. She just started to beat me up again, throwing me across the room.'

Sandra was kicked out of home and ended up sleeping on her friends' floors for a few months, went to her granny's for a few nights, then ended up back home again at her mum's. 'We had a huge row and she kicked me out for the very last time. I went to London's West End with a friend and slept rough on the streets for a while. My mind was dead, I was cracking up. My friend did all the talking and really looked after me.'

Sandra spent the weeks learning how to survive and trying not to be consumed by the vice and villainy that stalks young prey out in the open. 'We survived by begging, it was the only way to earn any money to eat, as benefits are impossible to get hold of. I kept on being arrested though, which was horrible. They would say awful things like "You dossers, why don't you get a job", or, "I bet you're on the game". It made me feel sick. One time we got arrested when my friend was begging and accepted a ten-pound note a CID woman was flashing at her. We were kept in a cell for a while because I refused to let her take all the blame. They tried to force us back home, but we couldn't, so we went straight back on to the street begging for food again!'

Sandra split up from her friend periodically, but they always somehow found each other again. 'My friend managed to get us off the street for a few weeks into a young persons' hostel. She met up with some other people and I ended up moving by myself into another hostel. It was run by nuns, which I didn't like at all. It was so strict, with early curfews. I was supposed to pray upstairs in a little church. But even though I was brought up to believe, I don't believe. Why would a god let all these bad things happen? The nuns were trying their best to help, but they were trying to brainwash me at the same time. I met up with my friend again and I left.'

Sandra and her mate slept back on the streets and this is where she met Paul. 'My friend went off with her boyfriend and just left me with Paul. Paul let me sleep out with him. He didn't try anything, he was like a big brother to me. We survived because Paul was an unbadged *Big Issue* seller and it was a quick way of making money without begging.'

Sandra and Paul became officially badged up vendors for *The Big Issue* and became financially independent. They also attended *The Big Issue's* writing workshop. 'Before when I used to write anything, I used to think it was silly and tear it up. At the writing group, people would say that my poetry was good and that I should carry on. Since then I have written over 250 poems. Once I write about something that has happened to me, it is like it's out of my mind. I feel happy.

'When other people read my poetry, they sometimes tell me that similar things have happened to them, with their parents. They say they wish their thoughts inside would leave them.

'Writing has brought my confidence back and is helping me understand words I didn't understand before. I also picked up a camera and started photographing people for the 'Capital Lights' section of *The Big Issue*. This way I have got to meet and talk to people in a way I would never have done before, whilst learning technical skills at the same time. I've now got a job at reception at *The Big Issue*, and slowly I'm breaking free into the big wide world. I have started doing a secretarial course part-time, which hopefully will lead to being a PA for someone.

'Paul and I did eventually get together. He really understands me, but I also understand him. Like my mother, he had a drink problem, which I helped him overcome. He had to for our relationship to survive. We moved from the bed and breakfast and we are now living in a rented flat. Paul became the editor of the 'Capital Lights' section of *The Big Issue* and we are engaged to be married, which for both of us, is a big commitment.

'When I look back, I didn't really know what being homeless was, until I was homeless myself. I just thought it happened to old men. I really believed if it ever happened to me I would kill myself. It is shocking to see so many ordinary people out there. If the government listened to those who have actually been homeless, they would see that *The Big Issue* is part of the answer, and that people can help themselves if they are helped.'

Sandra sees society's problems reflected in her family life, and in spite of the past has now found real hope. 'My new stepdad is really great, he really understands. He's more caring than my mum. I call him Dad. But I wish my mum would have more time for me and that she doesn't do to my sister what she did to me. I'm sure my mother's parents did the same to her when she was little. I've got to break the cycle when I start a family. I hope my mother shows me some real love before that happens.'

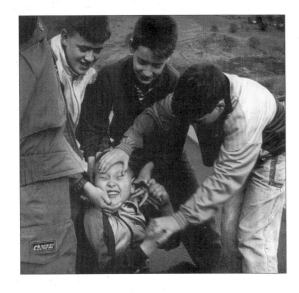

Top left
  Truancy, Salford, 1986.
Top right
  Attending school, Hampstead, London, 1985.
Bottom left
  Boys bullying after school, Aberfan, 1990.
Bottom right
  Boys bullying, secondary school, Herefordshire, 1985.

Violent boy, Salford, 1986.

BAD DREAMS

Bad dreams I have of you,
why did you do those
things to me?

You were supposed to look
after me,
like your own little girl.

Mummy doesn't know yet,
but she will find out,
soon,

I always feel dirty,
and that it's all my
fault.

But, Daddy you know it's all,
your fault,

People are after you, Daddy,
for what you did to me,

you're sick.

Why did you do it,
Mummy was there for you.

I was only a baby,
I didn't know what it meant.

You kept telling me that it was
our little secret.

I was too scared to tell her,

you made me bleed,
I hurt for days,
I was sick at school.

Why did you run away,
were you scared that I'm bigger now,
not a little girl any more.

You'll never find me now,
you're dead in my mind
and you always will be.

Your darling boy done it
to me too,

what's wrong with your family,

if I was you I'd stay away,
because when I find you
I'll kill you,
myself.

You don't know what it's been like,
the pain,
the hurt I had inside.

Sandra Clifford

THE BIG GREY HOUSE

The big grey house,
is where she lives,
she sits in her chair all day long,
and all night,
drinking her favourite drink.

Her child runs round
with no control,
while her mum sits there drinking away.

She promised me that she would give up,
But how could I be sure.

She sits there and cries,
and blames it on me,
but what have I done?
It's all in her head.

Sandra Clifford

THE CRACK IN THE WINDOW

Through the crack in the window
I can see all the poverty
that's going on inside.

Children starving to death,
but what do I do,
people sleeping rough,
what do I do.

People dying all over the world,
not enough money or food,
or help,
but what do I do.

Sandra Clifford

AS I

As I lay on my bed,
looking at the pouring rain,
I really mean the tears that run down my face.

As I write poems about the rain,
I usually think of all the bad
things

which have happened to me,
but when I think of all the happy times I have had
I start to smile and then I feel the happiness inside
shine across my face.

Sandra Clifford

YOU'RE

You're the one for me in
December,
you're the one for me,
whatever the month.

I love it when we cuddle up together,
December was such a wonderful month for me,
spending my first Christmas with you.

I'll give you one guess who I love,
yes it's you.

Sandra Clifford

CALLING YOU DAD

Calling you Dad but not knowing who I am,
doing it,
laying on the sofa in your
arms.

One minute I am fine the next
minute I am scared,
and alone.

You shout out loud,
and tell me off,
but it's not my fault,
that my head can see him.

Keeping daddy's secret,
kept inside for
far too long.

Sandra Clifford

Julia Swallow, Homelessness Prevention Officer for the government's Urban Programme Scheme which is being cut back nationally by £500 million pounds.

WATCHING THE MOON BEAMS

Watching the moon beams
Watching them fall
Crashing down on the
Ground

The sun doesn't come out
And we're walking in darkness
Feeling black and cold
Inside

Watching the stars in the
Sky twinkle and glow in
The blackness that overlooks
My room.

Sandra Clifford

THE DOORS

The doors that close behind me
Are the doors of my thoughts,
Pulling away the thoughts of
Bad

And thinking of the thoughts
Of good,
Sitting in this chair
Drifting away,

Pulling the doors behind
Me.

Thinking of how many times
You have shut those doors
Behind you.

As I sit here thinking,
Well that's what I usually
Do.

I think to myself,
Hiding for so
Many years,

Not showing the real
Person in me.

Sandra Clifford

Jason hitching to London, Haverford-West, Wales, 1991.

Three runaway young women, Centrepoint hostel, Soho, London, 1993.

Joan, Whitechapel, London, 1993.

Runaway missing boy, Soho, London 1993.

top left
    Young man about to spend his first night in a car park,
    London, 1993.
top right
    Homeless young man, Charing Cross Road, London, 1993.
bottom left
    Ex-prostitute, London, 1993.
bottom right
    Yoko, Ross and Max (their dog), the Strand, London, 1993.

Couple's joy after Neal (left) was successfully placed with gay foster parents by the National Association of Young People In Care (NAYPIC) - Neal was made homeless after being bullied by his father and brother, 1993.

Sky

Sky was born in 1967. He wants to take life as far as he dares possible. He does so with a sense of arrogance and gritted determination, leaving a trail of battles, most of them lost, until recently.

Sky was born in south London in 1967. His family moved to Oxford as his father was working for the Ministry of Defence, and on to Reading as his mother got a job in a bank. Sky's education was quite ordinary until he went to a naval boarding school. After leaving he decided that that the navy was not to be his career. Sky got his first temporary job in 1983 and from there things started to go down hill. He experienced crime and drugs on a small scale, but it left an indelible memory on his parents who thought that he had gone astray.

'I just wanted to peep over the fence, since nothing else was going right and I liked it until I was caught. Initially I was impressed by that other world of criminal freedom.'

The rebellion finally culminated at the end of 1986 with him leaving for London and independence. London was a huge place and frightening. 'I began to wonder what I had got myself into. When I saw the place, there were so many people I wondered whether I was going to survive. I was just looking for my little street paved with gold and happiness.'

For the next three years Sky worked as a courier and made progress. 'I was determined I was going to be good at something and I chose riding a bike for a living. It was like touching

inside yourself to find out what was achievable in testing the human mind and body. It was a total buzz.'

During the early winter of 1988 things started to go wrong. Sky explains, 'I had just lost the squat, the bike and the job. Nobody cared whether I lived or died, so I chose to die. Fortunately, though, suicide didn't work.'

Sky recovered, but his experiences left a long indelible scar on his memory. His mind contained fleeting glimpses of street homelessness and images of a stay in a remand centre during 1987.

Sky returned to London during the summer of 1989. He explains his initial feelings of freedom: 'It seemed the best time of my life, I was really going for it. I was 'speeding' continually and earning lots of money. But the squat where I ended up in came to an end and I found myself homeless and in the depths of the 'Bullring'. I suppose I was more prepared, but it still came as a shock to the system. I spent four weeks on the street until a friend found me and helped me off. It took a long time to recover, but I was willing to try again to rebuild my life.'

In April 1990 Sky found himself homeless and depressed again, but this time without the energy to help himself. 'I had burnt out, I guess I just couldn't get myself kick started again. Couriering was a no go because the money had gone. I just gave up and wondered what was going to happen next. I remember catching a quarter to four tube train from Ealing Broadway and arriving in a doorway on the Strand. I could have chewed everybody's head off if they were to come near me. I was very angry.'

It was at this time Sky started to write poetry starting with 'The London Streets'. 'I didn't even know what a poem was supposed to look like. I didn't know I was writing it. It was just like, Oh there's something interesting, let's write about

it! The poetry just happened. I didn't know whether it was good or not, but people seemed to like it.'

Sky's poetry ran like a diary and continues today as an accumulation of his feelings and the observations that make an impact on his life. Its importance is that he can get them out of his system quickly.

Some of his poems are witnesses to a chaotic period in Sky's life. During August 1990 he attempted suicide again, but was caught and sectioned as a danger to himself. 'I spent three weeks under section. It was the worst time of my life. When I wasn't stoned on the drugs they gave me, I was under constant security so I couldn't move anywhere. At night on the bridge, it wasn't a cry for help. I didn't want any help, I just wanted to die and a policeman stopped me. When they brought me into hospital I just screamed at everyone, including a social worker who was to change my life. To this day, shrinks can never figure me out because they are wrapped up in their books and labels. Eileen, my social worker, was and still is, the best person in the world. She is the only person who has ever had the real power to help me. I trust and respect her totally.'

When Sky came out of hospital, he got his first bedsit, which was in Paddington. He had mixed feelings and felt lost. 'I felt stuck in between the street and society and almost buried under - a motorway. Sadly Sky drifted into hard drugs. It was at this time that he wrote 'First Hit', about heroin. The only thing that kept him going was his involvement in his poetry and ultimately the publishing of his and other poets' work in a booklet titled 'An Act of Silence'.

'I learnt how to use a computer at a homeless day centre, the London Connection. At first I had no idea of the importance in putting together something which would make mine and other poets' lives visible. I managed to get a

grant from The Prince's Trust by just walking into their offices and demanding it. We printed 250 copies and distributed it to bookshops throughout London. When it was published it was like standing naked before the public and saying, "Now, judge me"?'

The booklet was a success, totally selling out and causing ripples which would benefit Sky later on. Sky eventually managed to kick the smack with Eileen's help, but he did relapse, then slowly started to recover again.

John Bird (*The Big Issue*'s editor) discovered Sky and his work, and cajoled him to be one of *The Big Issue*'s first vendors. By August, Sky received a massive boost by being allowed to form the first 'Capital Lights' section for *The Big Issue*. 'Capital Lights' was Sky's third poem and the homeless section was subsequently named after it. Sky went on to contribute many articles to the magazine and still writes to this day.

'*The Big Issue* was the saving of my life and I have a lot to thank the magazine. I did manage to sell it for a few months and earn enough money to get into night school. This led on to an application to university and a dream that I didn't even think about two years previously.'

Sky's application was successful and he was accepted into North London University to study for a degree in social policy. He has completed and passed his first year. At the time of his acceptance, his long awaited council flat came through and he now resides on a council estate in Queen's Park.

In a 'non-ending' conclusion, Sky has the last word. 'I have often wondered whether life does come full circle, and in fact I feel reborn with a new chance and outlook on life. I feel saddened today that many friends remain where I once was, and I pay tribute to the friends I have lost. I hope I will quietly take my place in society again, but I will never forget what happened in those homeless years. Indeed, I will never fully recover from the experience, but what I will say is that I have oddly benefited from it, in that it has made me a stronger person. I realize that you have nothing to lose in finding happiness, even if the journey includes some pain. At last, I have learnt how to lose that.'

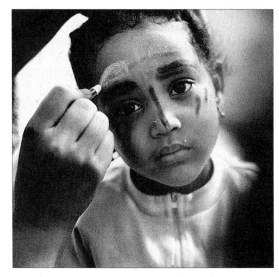

top left
  *Trish and Theresa in their 'Move-on-accommodation'
  (after staying at the 'Women's Direct Access Centre'),
  Liverpool, 1993.*
top right
  *Two abused women given refuge at the 'Women's Direct
  Access Centre' by the Liverpool Housing Dept who have
  prioritised women and bypassed uneconomical bed and
  breakfasts, 1993.*
bottom left.
  Trish in her new home-to-be, Liverpool, 1993.
bottom right
  *A child from one of the 1,300 Bayswater families and
  single people living in bed and breakfasts, at the
  Bayswater Hotel Homelessness Project - under continual
  threat of closure through cuts in social funding, 1993.*

Violent man (left) successfully treated at the Everyman Centre - now threatened with closure through shortfall of government money, 1993.

THE LONDON STREETS

A message goes out,
to the soulless people of power,
from the aggravated hearts
lying on the streets.

Fear not, we the homeless
seek drugs called salvation, happiness,
and hope.

We sit here on the streets
in cardboard cities,
in fear of people and
a reflected past.

My past no one wants to know,
I cringe in horror and pray to escape
to an unknown reality which is kind,
as night draws on.

We bring hopelessness to the streets.
A darkened form covering
our sins for being the wretched poor.

The privileged ignore the young.
Beware, it's around the corner.
Starvation, AIDS, and
the cold streets of London are real.
A world no one wants to enquire further into,
if they dare to.

Dreams are created
and die in an instant as morning dawns.
Hope withers as time goes on
with the creation of a fictitious world.

Time is our enemy.
Known only as a wasteland of death
on a devastating course of completing itself.
Haunting the occupants of the cold
London streets.

The streets scream - HELP!
before time digs a grave for me.
Please answer my plea of
Why me?

Sky
27th August 1990

FIRST HIT

I watch, fascinated.
The smack froths.
The first stage to obliteration.
My first hit.

Nervousness sweeps me.
I look away.
Scared.
Preparing.

Do I need it? I do.
Badly.
I need to escape
Rest and peace. Tormented.

I don't even feel it.
It slips painlessly in,
easing my memories.
My first hit.

I savour every moment.
My arm is warm.
A devastating instant.
I rush to my perfect world.

I think. What's the fuss?
I move.
I feel sick. Reality flickers.
HEROIN.

My mind talks to me,
my world slipping.
Time halts until
my eyes open.

I feel ill. Can't eat.
Was it all worth it?
Yes...I can control it.
Reality or imagination?

Sky
14th September 1990

EXTRACT FROM 'CAPITAL LIGHTS'

I wander beneath
the capital lights.
A beautiful city emblazoned
on my mind.

I think to myself, Why?
Reduced to such a low
to beg, to cry, to die
on the cold London streets.

I cry for myself.
I cry for the world,
so that people will see my rivers
and understand my pain.

Sky

Carla, Holloway Prison, 1993.

QUEEN OF HEARTS

A winter fantasy avenue;
To dream a life of love.
With warm blood flowing over a sea of
tenderness;
A winter escape to you, I run.

As cold winds fly to every direction;
With frost clinging to wings of angels;
I bring warmth of the heart;
To this merry Christmas.

Let me escape to fantasy lands;
Of princesses and poets;
With you as my queen;
The queen of hearts.
For I will love you soon.

Sky
19th December 1991

'Carla's past life', Holloway Prison, 1993.

A TEAR OF BLOOD

I hang under stars;
In judgement of apocalypse and beauty;
And seats of power twinkle;
In sight of my grave.

This is my final time,
To imagine about love, but none came;
And a trickle of blood,
Be my pain and a tear.

I judge you politicians,
For your lies and money.
My law is the emotion and the endurance,
Of what I loved...destroyed by you.

Time will watch me perish;
For I believed it would not savage my own
policies
Of blue skies and butterflies.

These words have now breathed;
The power of truth;   *i*
And I decree that you follow;
For I believe
And that won't die.

Sky
16th November 1990

THE DARKNESS HOURS

Time to live
Darkness approaches,
within an ever
gripping form.

When light gives way to darkness,
so the life changes to a
twilight of cruel reality
called survival.

Ashamed and embarrassed,
the occupants on the cold London streets
attempt to achieve their
nightly result of obliteration.

People walk past, ignoring.
Some flirt a glimpse,
afraid of an alternative nightmare.
Scared of living.

Pimps, cruisers, pushers and kerb-crawlers,
the night is theirs now.
Time to give in,
to a land of shattered dreams.

Lonely men stand on street corners.
Bearing testimony to
their addiction called
the streets of the West End.

They are the unseen angry.
They bear the burden of protecting
the young, crying because of
their conscience.

Dawn arrives.
Memories of night last added to the past.
Time passes quickly.
Must get ready for another night on the
streets.

Sky
27th July 1990

MY TWILIGHT FRONTIERS

I stand on fresh ground.
Unsteady, unsure of what I see.
Dream horizons of beauty and light
Is where I am looking.
Gone are my twilight frontiers of yesterday,
I really wanted to stay.

O'Darkness, O'Darkness;
I wanted you this morning,
A shadowy veil to cover my desperation,
To remain anonymous.
Something I am used to, O'Darkness,
A life my conscience doesn't see.

Soft lips of warmth herald a new dawn;
Of once was to become today.
A kiss, a touch, an avenue to ecstasy.

Love, an unknown echo to thrust forward;
Over my twilight frontiers,
Towards my dream horizons.

Sky
14th January 1992

'The Homeless Industry' - £85 per cubicle at the Christian Alliance Hostel, (80 per cent funded by the taxpayer), London 1993.

'The Homeless Industry' - £100 per bed at the Salvation Army Hostel, Cardiff. One resident is certified as undernourished.

top left
  Marion (care leaver), successfully fought for the funding of her philosophy and theology degree with the National Association of Young People In Care (NAYPIC) - hundreds of young care leavers are denied assistance in spite of the 1989 Children's Act.

top right
  Natasha (care leaver and NAYPIC worker) with her daughter, Porsha, after struggling with the authorities to secure permanent accommodation, Herne Hill, London, 1993.

bottom left
  'Generations of violence' - violent mother (who was hit by her father), Haverford-West, Wales, 1991.

bottom right
  Angela Banner, foster mother, with her own children, near Haverford-West, Wales, 1991.

Young person, Manchester.

Tay Devlin

Tay was born in 1942. His life has been both immensely rewarding and incredibly brutal. He bears a semi-permanent smile and a twinkle in his eye, which reveals a very endearing man. He has no self pity, and never minces his words. Tay's life story, of how he reached the streets, is both a boy-made-good dream and an unthinkable nightmare. Tay explains how he was a millionaire by the time he was thirty, making his money writing hit singles. By the time he was forty-seven, Tay was homeless. The route from fame and fortune to being penniless has been an immensely painful journey, especially for a man whose childhood was spent in a Barnardo's children's home.

'I never knew my real parents. I was brought up in Barnardo's and joined the army at the age of seventeen.

'I was marzipan, easy to manipulate. I had been in care all my childhood, so the army utilized all the anger I had within me and moulded me into a soldier. I thought I'd done well by getting into the army. Most of my friends went into some form of villainy.'

During his childhood, Tay learnt to survive as he knew how. 'I used to steal all the time, but it used to be practical things like food, torches, toothbrushes and books. I would secretly read under my covers at night. We were poor, very poor, so I learnt to be an efficient thief,

probably one of the best in London for my age. The army was just an extension of what I had learnt as a kid.'

Tay became a very proficient soldier, fighting in different parts of the world, often in extremely dangerous situations. Eventually he was badly hit and, in the operating theatre, had a near-death experience 'I was in a room, looking at my body laying facing down and I had total freedom to go anywhere I wanted. I had form, I had arms, I was there, but I wasn't encumbered by a body. I actually left the building and travelled, I could have gone anywhere I liked. But I panicked. The next thing I knew I was jumping, gasping for breath. If I had kept on travelling out of my body, I know someone would have found me dead.'

Tay has formed strong spiritual convictions, 'I think we come back to get it right. Anything can go wrong and we keep coming back until we make the world a better place. I can now see how I can play my part. Perhaps this was meant to happen, so I could learn.'

Tay left the army with £700, bought an E-type Jaguar and started driving around a band, 'The Tremeloes'. 'I used to strum songs on the guitar when I was in the army, but never thought anything would come of them. When I met The Tremeloes I gave them a song and it became a hit. It was that simple. From there I wrote for Desmond Decker and went over to Jamaica and worked with Bob Marley. It just happened, and I became a millionaire.

'I never knew what to do with my money. I had to have everything new. If a new Rolls-Royce came in, I would have to have it. I had too much jewellery, too much gold. I had a company worth sixteen million pounds. Quite a lot for a boy who had fuck all in 1971!

I handled it all wrong and naively. I was completely nouveau riche.'

In 1982, during the height of his music career, Tay got called back to serve in the Falklands campaign.'When I got the letter I was completely unfit. But I knew I had the expertise and I just saw it as another job. I dropped everything and went to work.'

Tay's perceptions of the war are expressed in his poem 'War and Peace'. 'I looked at an Argentinian kid who I took out who was eighteen or nineteen, I was forty. He was probably playing football the week before. A week later I blew his head off. I looked at him and thought: How grotesque, how sad, what a shame. He's got brothers, sisters, a family. Now he's gone. I'm there to do a job, but it's ministers and government who put you there. They're not in the mud, sweating, getting their brains blown out. The Argentinian kid was put there for exactly the same reasons as me.'

Tay came back from the Falklands and resumed his music career where he had left off. He shut away his experiences of war from his friends and girlfriend, and in 1983 he got married.

'The first person who gave me a perspective on my life was my wife who I nicknamed 'Shadow'. Shadow was always there, caring for me and loving me. Through her I learnt to love back for the first time in my life. She was a titled lady, wealthy in her own right, she loved me, warts and all. Shadow was also an amazing singer and together we wrote music and started a family. We produced two beautiful kids, a boy and girl, and fatherhood just seemed to come naturally. I was the happiest man in the world.

'I used to lark about with Shadow and my

children, climbing up trees, playing around, shouting and screaming around parks, kissing and cuddling. Doing all the things I never could do when I was little. We all really loved each other.'

Then, in October 1989, the unthinkable happened. Shadow finished recording a song with Tay at their home studio and said she would nip out with the kids to see her parents. Tay explains, 'It was an ordinary night, just an ordinary night. Then I had a knock on the door and the police told me that my wife and kids had been hit by a lorry pulling out into the fast lane on the motorway. The driver was drunk. My wife and kids hit the reservation and were killed outright by the traffic coming the other direction. It was a mess. The worst moment of my life was when I identified their bodies. To see them laying there, that's what destroyed me.

'I walked. I just walked. I hit the bottle and was completely numb. I left my boats, my mansions, my Lamborghini, Rollers - none of it mattered any more. Money was immaterial. Life was Shadow to me.'

Tay does not recall the first six months at all. 'My first impressions of the street were of oblivion. But I was fit enough, or hard enough, to survive. There is a pecking order out there, you have to establish yourself or forever be trodden on.'

Once Tay was known, he discovered the human side of street life. 'You make friends and discover a lot of humanity and warmth from the community, you just have to look for it or be lucky. If you want food you have to be up front of the line. I was OK, but if you're a woman out there it is doubly hard.

'With all my money, I never believed I was ever going to become homeless. There are people out there on the streets for all sorts of reasons. It could happen to anyone. The thing is we all need help, someone needs to do something about it. Many people just closed the door one day and bang, they became homeless. They just fell through the net. Perhaps they had a little company one day, went boss-eyed, lost their homes and ended up homeless. There are bankers, writers, photographers out there, it happens frighteningly quickly.'

Tay remembers how he once used to think of the homeless. 'I was completely condescending, I had no idea. I thought the homeless were a bunch of winos. It's ironic, because, I remember one night when I was at Stringfellow's, I must've spent a couple of grand on champagne and on having a good time. I picked up some sandwiches and ordered my chauffeur to stop the roller by the Strand, so I could throw off some sandwiches to the homeless. Little did I realize that I would end up there a couple of years later.

'I suppose none of us know. What do we know? My wife had no idea that she would be killed that day, and I never realized I'd end up homeless. Life's like that. I don't know now who was more dead, my wife or me. I'm fighting to stay alive and that way I can try and keep her and my babies alive.

'If I had my money back again I would build a huge hostel, especially for women, where they could shut the doors and temporarily live their lives how they want. I would build proper facilities until they were properly housed. You just can't rely on this government to do that. They just stick families in bed and breakfasts and don't give a damn. Out of sight out of mind, but they're still homeless. In the long term families need real homes. How is anyone supposed to live on £42 a week and still be able to love and care for their children? How can you bring up children like that and expect them not to fall into the same trap?

'I wrote a poem called 'Dosser'. I might call myself a dosser, but I wouldn't let anybody else. On the streets you don't live a day at a time, not an hour at a time but minute by minute. Life and death was on a knife edge; whether you'd eat, whether it would freeze that night, whether you'd be stabbed or given some food. Many people die on the streets. Life expectancy is only about forty-five years and I'm fifty. I just knew I had to get out of the cold and the degradation.'

Tay eventually got a place in a hostel and describes the incident which motivated him to get off the streets. 'I was an 'unbadged' *Big Issue* seller. I still had a huge drink problem. I looked terrible and just wanted money for my 'paradise'. I was still trying to obliterate all my memories and was just going further and further downhill.

'One day I just looked up and saw my old mate, Elton John, who recognized me. He was shocked to see me in such a bad way. He couldn't believe it. He said that my wife would never have wanted to see me looking so bad. Elton told me I should get off the booze and that I owe it to my wife and myself to sort my life out. I blatantly told him to piss off and leave me alone. He just stood and stared. I could see he understood, he'd been through exactly the same problem with the drink. He suggested that we go to an Alcoholics Anonymous meeting, and we did.

'I was drunk when I walked in. Elton hugged me. He was loving, I knew he really cared, and that really mattered. It was like when a baby duck first opens its eyes and what it sees becomes its mother. That was Elton for me. His name didn't matter, he could have been Reg Bloggs. His friendship made me realize I could begin again.'

Tay became a fully committed *Big Issue* vendor, which gave him a real sense of pride and direction, and this was when he first picked up a pen to write poetry. 'My first poem I wrote on the streets was called 'Flame'. I saw an amazing woman with red hair when I was vending outside the Body Shop. When she walked past she gave me a wonderful smile, and every time she would walk past, I would smile back. It was the first time I smiled for two and a half years. We got to talk and she was incredibly inspiring. I then felt a huge inclination to write, and out came my first poem. It was a letter to her, a cry for help.'

'Flame' was published in *The Big Issue*, which was a great moral booster and opened up new possibilities for Tay. He still sees 'Flame' while he vends. 'She still smiles, gives me a kiss now and again. She gives me hope. She lit up my life and now I've found a real direction.'

Tay is now in a hostel and is fighting to get back into mainstream society. 'I've had enough, I want to get a proper roof over my head. I've eased off the booze and I'm inspired. Words and melodies seem to flow as they used to, and I'm writing songs again. But If I make it this time I want to do something for the homeless. If I can write a song to achieve that, great. Someone's got to do something for the homeless, whatever the reason they are out there.'

'Tay's past life'

Homeless man, South Bank, London, 1993.

Single-parent mother, Stockwell, 1987.

top left
  'The return home'. One of the former mentally ill patients
  from Hackney Hospital, who continually return to its gates
  after release into the 'care in the community' programme.
  London, 1993.
top right
  'Care in the community', Herefordshire, 1986.
bottom left
  Jessica (with learning difficulties) and Sam, London, 199
bottom right
  Psychiatric institution with inadequate staff to patient
  provision, Herefordshire, 1986.

Homeless woman with learning difficulties - one of the 3,000 homeless in London with mental health problems, 1993.

'SHADOW'

'Shadow' was always there for me,
With me,
Next to me at all times.
I loved her so much,
I still do.
She, my little girl, my little boy,
Were killed in a car crash in '89.
A drunken lorry driver pushed them
Through a motorway barrier into
Oncoming traffic.
They burnt to death.
Somewhere in the world someone
Whose son I killed could say
'Fair justice'.
I will see my darlings again
And no doubt the people that
I have 'moved on',
I hope we will all be at peace.
I quit the system for some three years.
My regiment looked after me.
My Government did not.
I now sell The Big Issue
I am moving forward again,
On and on.
Upwards,
Relentless.
I have to win.

Tay Devlin

O' NO

Butterflies look so pretty
Were they always so?
O' no.

Weld your tongue to your cheek
You say too much.
O' no.

You never did argue with a loaded gun.
I did!
O' no.

God is calling me,
I won't go.
O' no.

Shit I'm here.
O' no.

Tay Devlin

FIRE IN MY HEART

Tears drop upon a velvet skin
I never wanted to be there again
Broken dreams I feel you fear
I'm coming closer to feel you near
I give thanks to the fire.

The spoken word the stolen heart
I never want us to be apart
The touch of faith beyond our control
It's buried deep within our souls
And I pray to the fire.

Tay Devlin

EXTRACT FROM 'WAR AND PEACE'

I have pride to lean on.
My regiment
My country.
Another hit.
Nice one son.
I'm getting the flavour now.
Waste who I meet in this place.
I must win.
Strange.
Maybe in a pub I meet drink with them.
Laugh.
Joke.
Talk.
But now,
Gun in hand, I move on.
Creating hell.
Here to work.
Kill.
Stop all that challenges me.
Man.
Animal.
Machine.
God even.
What am I?
I'm dangerous!
Bad news for those who oppose.
I am here.
I'm good.
Very good.
Too good for most.
I feel nothing at all!
Do I?
Life is black and white
Another picture show?
Am I one of the players?
I kill again.
Just look at the twisted tortured body.
Lifeless.
Grotesque really
Oozing red.
Flesh shattered.
I sit and clean my guns.

Scaning deep into the rain.
His unseeing eyes stare at the night
I see where the stars touch the earth.
He cannot.
Yes.
I am here
Another life extinct.
There are flowers in this field.
So nice
So soft.
White
Pink
Blue
I like blue
My favourite colour
It was him or me
Or others
Blood is blue
Turns red when exposed to oxygen
I turned all the flowers red.
Not with oxygen
I eat.
Movement.
Gun jams.
Clear it.
Death for me yet?
Kill or be killed.
All is fair in love and war.
So they say.
War?
Love?
I kill.
I smile.
No warmth, eyes are so cold.
Again I kill.
Goodbye to all whom I meet in this place.
Did I send a birthday card for my son?
Ministers.
Governments.
Rules.
Loyalty.
What put me in this place?

Tay Devlin

Billy (homeless) and his Gauguin picture. Billy is one of the 70 per cent of offenders released from prison who offered no form of accommodation (even though he applied). He is back again for stealing, after he couldn't find work and his dole money ran out. Brixton Prison. 1993.

'FLAME'

Walked by me again today
She smiled
Head erect.
So elegant.
Red hair flowing.
As flames from the sun
Her skin like silk.
Her smile so warm
Lilt in her voice
Sent shivers down spine
Her eyes so pure
There is pain
She hides it well
Her walk
Her manner
Her movement
Her class
Her style
Jeans, skirt or dress
She shines through
Perfection in motion
A vision
A dream
I'll call her 'Flame'
So pretty
Can I have these feelings?
Three years
Alone in darkness
Call it hell.
The preacher said a prayer tonight
For my departed loves
I said amen.
Nearly a tear came
Being a man
I cannot cry

Then I mentioned 'Flame'
Do I love her?
Am I too old?
Too ugly?
Too scared?
Can I climb back to the top?
She is a vision of beauty
A dream
Her presence
Stops the lonely winds that chill
My heart
Does she know?
How beautiful she is
Could I just hold her?
Touch hands
Smooth brow
Gently hold
Kiss?
Caress
Brush her hair for hours on end
Just look
Drink in her beauty
No!
You fool
She is too perfect to touch
A goddess.

Tay Devlin

DOSSER

Air is still free
So today I breathed.
My eyes are silent
But I still see
My heart is under your bed.
Is Marc Bolan really dead?
I need some love
Is my vocabulary so bad
I have to profane?
Fuck life!!
Why am I here?
Have I done all the things I say?
Is it just a dream?
Music soothes the savage beast.
Play Elvis
Play Beatles
Take 'Mikado' into the war zones
In doorway I lie
Cardboard box
Foetus position
Why?
Life is a gold packet
Life is a gold can
Beg a drink
Beg a coin.
Give me an answer God
'Cause here I am.
On the street
A dosser
Am I really damned?

Tay Devlin

Homeless young man, Jason, having just caught a sparrow with his hand. Haverford-West, Wales, 1991.

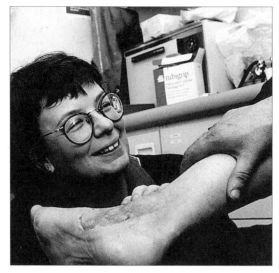

top left
Harmonica player, Lincoln's Inn Field, London, 1993.
top right
One of the few national primary health care nurses, at the excellent St. Botolph's homeless centre, London, 1993.
bottom left
Michael Halford had both legs amputated after suffering from frostbite whilst sleeping rough, University College Hospital, London, 1993.
bottom right
Couple waiting four more months for their child to be born. Sleeping rough on the 'Bullring', South Bank, London, 1993.

Homeless man with a suspected heart attack, the City, London, 1991.

Lizz Knight

Lizz's exact age remains a secret, and until now so has her turbulent life. Lizz spent virtually twenty years on and off the street, becoming a mother figure to many young people finding themselves homeless. Lizz spent most of her time at St Martin-in-the-Fields, where she has written prolific quantities of poetry and nurtured many lost souls. Lizz's own life is filled with tragedy, but she has always been an inspiration with her words and generous smiles. The time has come however, to discover the woman behind the smile.

Lizz was born on an RAF base in Jordan. She and her family remained there for seven years until being transferred to Germany, where they stayed for another two years before arriving in Cyprus. The family stayed for a further three years before returning to the UK, when her father was suddenly discharged.

'I can't remember too much of my childhood, up to the age of sixteen when my father died. I took it very badly and after deciding I would be a burden on my mother, I left home. After travelling awhile, I finally reached London during 1971. By this time I was suffering severe depression and there was no real housing

support, so I just slipped out onto the streets.'

For the next fourteen years, until 1985, Lizz remained on the street. She was accepted into the homeless community as one of their own. 'At that time the street was the only place where I wasn't treated as an outcast. The Seventies were different to the Eighties and Nineties,' Lizz explains, 'In those days we looked after each other and nobody pushed themselves on nobody. Today it's totally changed.'

Lincoln's Inn Fields was London's homeless heartland and 'Cardboard City' (before it was transferred to the South Bank, during the mid-Eighties). It was a real community and Lizz played a large part in what was going on. 'The centre of conversation was the bandhouse. At night, bonfires would light up the surrounding buildings as we tried to keep warm. There were the casualties during winter, like the alcoholics who died because they couldn't drink any more. Most were my friends.'

Many young runaways would arrive at Lincoln's Inn Fields and Lizz would take them under her wing and teach them the basics of survival, whilst listening to their problems. 'They were little tearaways in those days. I could see myself in them because I knew exactly how they felt. But, I knew I was no replacement. What they really needed was someone to love them and I couldn't do that, I did my best to protect them though.'

Today most of the young homeless steer clear of the veterans, but Lizz receives

many visits from the teenagers she helped during the Seventies. She takes a great comfort that her time on the streets hasn't been an entire waste.

During 1985, her life did take a good turn. Lizz met and married an ex-homeless guy and together they moved to Manchester. 'It was the happiest day of my life. I really thought I was on the way to what you consider a normal life. How wrong I was.'

Over the next eighteen months, Lizz gave birth to two children and the house took shape. Unfortunately, her husband started to drink heavily; after a while, Lizz drank as well. In 1987, after fights and arguments, the marriage came to its conclusion and the kids went to a sister.

'I returned to London badly smashed up inside, I just hit the bottle, I couldn't handle it. Perhaps I was hoping too much that I could change so fast in trying to adjust. I will never dare to hope that much again.

'I knew my place was on the street and I knew I had to find a place for my pain and anger, and that was my poetry.' Lizz had started writing poetry in 1985. Until now she has not shown her work to anyone except at the St Martin-in-the-Fields homeless centre. Lizz makes no apologies for 'its brutal beauty'. Lizz goes on to describe, 'It was the only place I could be brutal with my thoughts with any sense of privacy. I had given up. I didn't care any more. If people saw me as a problem, it was their problem and what they wanted to see.'

Lizz moved back into Lincoln's Inn Fields and spent the next three years as an alcoholic. Her poetry showed visions of mental flashbacks during this period. 'My poetry almost acted as a trigger, it was like therapy. My poems were like a battleground of thoughts, where I could eventually console my memory and find a future direction.'

During 1990, Lizz moved into a homeless shelter up in Nottingham, and stayed in the town for a year. 'I went to get away from it all and to get some fresh air. I got the break and I kicked the drink, but couldn't get on my feet again and found it difficult to form relationships with people. They say I have got psychiatric problems. To me it washes over my head. I have strong spiritual beliefs, and I believe this has carried me through all the ups and downs and has helped me form positive backgrounds for my poetry.'

When Lizz returned to London it was to the streets. 'I find London hard, too hard. The streets are no place for anyone, let alone women or children.' Because of this view, Lizz is now back in Nottingham. She explains, 'I know my future lies in making a go of it and trying to start life afresh, out of danger.

'My poems are now about a better world where people don't harm each other or our environment. They are about how we could all live together if we tried, without poverty or homelessness. Just peace.'

107

'Graffiti statement', 1993.

Homeless young man, London, 1991.

REMEMBER THE WORLD

Remember this: but for the grace of God
There would not be mankind.
God made this world we live in.

God made all beautiful things you see
How long the world lasts is up to you
The future of this land is in your hands.

So come on, wake up before it's too late
Before the world becomes grey and black.
Put some life back in the land.

But for the grace of God
We would have no animals or trees
This world would be very bare.

Remember. The earth is a living thing.
It's something to care about.
The future is in your hands now.

Lizz Knight

TREES, 1992

We trees would love to speak out
The pain we would say, of all the rain.
The pain of the axe chopping us down.

Think of what you do to us.
We were here before you came;
We stood tall and proud.

Now we stand here in shame
And look at you and you with your acid rain
To see the hurt and pain.

You do not care what happens to us.
You say, 'Tree, what are you to me?'
We trees have feelings too.

Think before you do what you have to do.
We ask you not to kill us.
We were here long before you came.

Lizz Knight

ALONE DID STAND

Alone as a hill did stand
Oh - oh - a wolf so grand
Just as the moon high in the sky.

Then did a mighty cry out loud come.
That wolf was off on the run.
To find its mate or the pack.

A hunting that wolf did go.
Where it went I do not know.
Yet in the moon a farmer cried.

'My flock is one less today.
That wolf has been back again,'
The farmer he did cry out loud.

Tonight I will watch when the moon is high
Yes, that wolf was on the hill,
Farmer said, 'Tonight, wolf you die.'

Lizz Knight

Homeless man begging, London, 1992.

I KNOW A PLACE, 1992

I know of a place so peaceful
Where I can be on my own
It is high up in the mountains

The place is very quiet
It is off the beaten track
No one will ever find me.

In this place of peacefulness
With a river and waterfall
I know that I can rest

A place that time's forgotten
A place that I can sit and think
If only I did own this place

If only I did own this place
That time has long forgot
No one would ever find me.

Lizz Knight

THE CAVE

I went for a walk along the coast
Down the cliff path I found a cave.
It was not a smugglers' cave at all.

This cave was someone's home.
A bed, a lamp also a lot of books.
It looked so very clean inside.

Along the cave wall holes were dug.
Just like the shelves at home.
As I began to leave a person did appear.

This person was a little old man.
He said, 'Please stay a little while.
Talk to me and let me know what is new.

You see I have lived down here so long
I do not know what is going on.
You see you are the only one who knows I'm
here.'

Lizz Knight
18th June 1992

YEARS AWAY FROM HOME

It is years that I have been gone.
No more do I know that town
It has changed so much now.

I never felt so lost before
The silence as I pass people by
It does not feel like my old home town.

Faces I never saw before
People I do not know at all
I do not feel at all safe.

This is what happens when you're away
People you once knew are long gone.
It has changed so much.

The pleasure of returning home,
I was wrong to return to that town.
No one I know was left in that town.

Lizz Knight
17th June 1992

A NEW WORLD SO FAR AWAY

This new world so far away
Not like this earth today
A new world a place of peace.

A world with lots of love
Not like this world today
A world without hurt or shame.

A world with love and lots of care
A world without sorrow and wars
A world without hunger.

A world with peace and lots of homes
A new world without homelessness
A new and better world.

This world is out there somewhere
Way beyond our star it is there
This world is where I want to live.

Lizz Knight
7th March 1993, 2AM.

'Oblivion.' Glue-sniffing, Cardiff, 1993.

top left
   Dai, street performer/actor, and friend in his squat, Shepherd's Bush, 1993.
top right
   The Big Issue drama workshop, Victoria, London, 1993.
bottom left
   Yassin, ex-homeless, with her 'Childhood Painting', Cardiff City Youth Project (recently financially reprieved - for the time being), 1993.
bottom right
   John, homeless busker, South Bank, 1993.

Fred, son of Yvette and Michael Mansfield QC, London, 1993.

Woman found innocent after spending nine months in prison 'on remand' - many lose homes, partners, or jobs as a result. London, 1993.

Alf Welton

Alf was born in 1953. For the last twelve years, Alf has been a nomad in London. His poetry is his vision of an upside-down world. Alf believes his security lies in having no home and he defends his 'choice', which many tabloid newspapers have historically condemned as 'sponging'. Alf speaks few words and his vision of society is perceived in poems which are beautifully sharp and until now, apart from the homeless community, have been unknown.

Alf was born in Hackney, East London. His family moved to Liverpool when he was two and for the next twenty-five years he remained in that city. Alf speaks sparingly about his childhood, albeit about the poverty generally in the city. 'The prospects then, as now were exceptionally difficult, with no real jobs to speak of and little to do.

'I didn't have a very good childhood. It was tough in those days living with the parents for that period of time. It was the late Seventies. There were no jobs and basically I think I became part of a lost generation, forever wandering in my mind. In fact I think things today are a bit easier, but not much. I look back and think, well at least I had two parents. But, when they split, I just left.'

Alf arrived in London sometime in 1981. He is not sure precisely when. His objective of getting a job was unfortunately never reached. Alf

remained on the streets for the next twelve years, and resides there today.

Alf regards himself as a 'dosser' and therefore not homeless. He explains, 'Never call me homeless because I never would, or want to, fit into that social category of the younger kids on the streets and their problems. Most of them only need a bit of attention shown to them. They don't really fit in to the streets at all. I'm sure they don't want to stay there either. That's the definition of homelessness. I know there are a lot of mentally ill on the streets and that is unfair. What choice have they got? Hospital, hostel, or the street. Anyway, I want to be on the streets, and I can be called a dosser because it is a way of life. There is a certain freedom. I must say though that our numbers have been cut down, but any which way you look at it, we want to stay. Simple. Mind you, things have changed, there isn't the comradeship any more. It's a pity.'

Alf describes himself as a man without direction. 'Years seem to pass by and I just watch as another decade is beginning. I watch change occurring and I just don't want to be disturbed. I can't understand why society continually tries to persuade me that I should join in. I've tried and failed, now just let me observe.

'I think that if I was to take part in the rat race, I would be a sponge vegetable. It may sound like an excuse by not going with the flow, but I don't think it is an excuse, it's the truth. For me anyway. I think we are all going too fast and not liking it. As a society, do we really put ourselves and the family first or the greater good? I wonder what the definition of happiness is? I certainly have fun looking for

one. Please look around you, we're all exhausted!' Alf sees his life as a constant wonder, from one new experience or beautiful view to another. He explains that his definition of his situation is reflected in his poetry. His vision goes behind the obvious or immediate, into a place of constant beauty. To Alf it is an escape to a perfect world, of being a fly on the wall, watching people and environments go by. Alf's sanity is preserved by being an outsider, perhaps an existentialist. Alf never takes drink or drugs, so he can't be stereotyped and he shouldn't be classified for what he likes or observes.

Alf loves reading Japanese poets, because of their deep sense of history and culture. To Alf, poetry will always remain as an art, as it does to them.

'My work should be about beauty and love and my poems should only be viewed as a vision, like a picture in words. Believe me, if you can describe a picture in words, you have done a good job in explaining what you see.'

Alf's years on the streets have taken an exacting toll on his health and he admits he doesn't look after himself. Alf is resolute though, that he will spend the rest of his days living rough. 'I know the system back to front, you have to, to survive. I can't regret what I have never had, so I'm happy being free.'

At the time of writing, Alf is residing in a short-term hostel for the homeless. He has been there for the last six weeks, having a rest before returning and spending another summer on the streets.

'I'm having a holiday at the moment and

having a good laugh.' Alf will return and do what he is good at, and that is being a fly on the wall of society and chuckling all the time.

Homeless man, (denied the right to vote), Ladbroke Grove, London, 1993.

WINTER RHYME

Clouds are white
Days are short
No more light
Darkest night

Seastorms blow
Ships are tossed
White rivers flow
Moving snow

Black bull snores
Red cows low
Wild wind roars
High hawk soars

Red fern stays
Earth grasps roots
Shady lays
Foxes' ways

Wild geese fly
Bare trees sway
Seagulls cry
Clouds race by

Hoarfrost chills
Rime on stone
Snow capped hills
Daunted wills

Hang up hood
Inside hut
Hearth is good
Fire eats wood.

Alf Welton

LINCOLN'S INN FIELDS, 1:42AM

Somewhere near glass shatters on stone
Tongues corkscrew in a wringing of spite.
Complicated Mongolian syllables fall
From archless mouths who suffer
Beneath star-flowering nightclouds.

Wind-bothered litter-fires flicker against fathoms
Of dark legends, while strange lucent hands
Reach out from shadowy cripples
And warm themselves in the orange glow.
Little hell in a wastebasket.

Alf Welton

LINCOLN'S INN FIELDS, 2:02AM

Watching zeros cramp into an unidentifiable
Sourness. Untouchable uneradicable.
Sliding like age, then disappearing, into collapsing
Rectangles through whose cardboard walls
I locate death rattles in the spaces
Of a motherless geometry.

Alf Welton

LINCOLN'S INN FIELDS, 2:27AM

Summer has turned its back forever
On this place of no forces.
O sulphurous meadow, kingdom and shackle,
The buttercups have gone.

Alf Welton

Rally for the homeless, Trafalgar Square, London, 1993.

OCCIDENTAL DEATH

Sun sinking
beyond a purple range.
Evanescent dream.
All else continues.
Stars shine
in an oriental sky.
Butterfly settling
on wine-flecked
saffron petals,
shaking the dust from its wings.
Impudent blackbird carrying
the gold of sunset on his back.
Beneath the maples swaying creaking limbs,
shadows dance and lengthen
on the windswept grass.
Enchanted murmurings.
Above a fiery red, heavenly wound
O burning bloody western sky:
if, like my eyes,
my heart too,
could touch a hurt like that!

Alf Welton

OLD WOMAN, QUITE MAD, IN A FOG

Diffusing light - all around
Grey veil,
Whose coolness, whose wetness
Touched her, beneath her skin.

Deep deep set eyes:
Persecuted cloisters standing
Amid the ruins
Of a many times sacked
Renegade monastery.

Closely guarded secrets
Now passing, phantom-like between
Rime-eaten columns, vaporous
As the mist surrounding
That bloodless tragedy - her face.

Her face. Colourless.
Her thoughts droplets
On an abandoned spider's web.
Shaken loose by haunting echoes.
Somebody else's footsteps.

Aching expanded eyes fixed.
Fragmenting stained glass pleading
Silently
Grey on black.
How it stood out!

That grey worm - like a hair
On her black shawl.
It refused to go away.

She felt. She thought.
Briefly. Eternally
That this was not the way
She, an impossible she,
Would like to be remembered!

Alf Welton

TO A.R.

I want to be the seed you steal,
From the blackberry bush,
To secretly celebrate the coming of summer.
I want to be the flower you pick
And hold close to your breast
For just a breath, a whisper,
A single beat of your heart.
I want to be the answer and the quiet
You seek and wish for
In those troubled moments.
I want to be the hymn you sing
To him. The one.
I am the cry of a bird
From a desolate place.
I am the singer who comes
To sing you a dreadful song
In the night. A starless night.
I am a bitter burning flame.
Still and silent in an endless void.
I am sleep banished.
I am seen yet unheard.
Near yet untouchable.

Alf Welton

ALISON IV

From the nightingale
Comes the song of the darkest hour

From the daughters of the wind
Comes Alison, dancing,
With Aurora's bright charm.

With her first gentle breath
The opening of the lilies
Her sweet bouquet, rising, then
Dispels the grey from the sky.

Alf Welton

top left
  Boys by 'For Sale' signs in Notting Hill Gate - there were 68,500 house repossessions in 1992.
top right
  Executive Job Club, Birkbeck College, London, 1993.
bottom left
  Big Issue vendor, London, 1993.
bottom right
  Company liquidator Richard Kravetz, handling the insolvency of Portman Lamborghini - one of Britain's 22,938 insolvencies in 1992.

Commuter, South Bank, London, 1993.

Photo-montage, 1993.

top left
  School children, Rhymney Valley, South Wales, 1985.
top right
  Anti-nuclear graffiti suggesting opposition to Britain spending tax payers' money (£23 billion pounds)on the Trident nuclear system, Vauxhall, London, 1990.
bottom left
  Robert Green (Ex-RN Commander), part of a worldwide campaign 'The World Court Project' to legally abolish nuclear weapons (based on the successful abolition of slavery) - resulting in a massive release of finance to develop social programmes worldwide.
bottom right
  Rally for the homeless, London, 1993.

Louise Ambridge

Louise was born in 1974. She has something very rare that many of us lack and that is innocence. She very much wants to hang on to it for the rest of her life in her quest for happiness. However, innocence is a very dangerous virtue to have in trying to find the elusive 'right' partner. A relationship with a man, whether he is a lover, husband or father, can be the cause of great pain. Where parents sometimes fail, the longing for someone to love and be loved by is often a cry for help or plea for understanding. Sadly, in the process, innocence can be badly dented or crushed. Somehow Louise has survived.

At the time of writing, Louise has her own bedsit in a town called Barry, twelve miles from Cardiff, and is near to where she was born and brought up. Louise has one brother and three sisters; she is the oldest. Her parents have only known unemployment benefit since jobs are nonexistent in Barry. Her problems started in her early teens.

'My mum was and still is an alcoholic and mum and dad used to fight a lot. I always used to fight my mum but not my dad. I liked him because he could always stand back as an outsider almost, and say either I was wrong or mum was. Mum would have a go just for the sake of having a go.'

At the age of thirteen, Louise entered her teenage crisis or rebellion period and this was

when her mother rejected her and she was placed in care. 'I was thirteen and I was going through the usual teenage thing, like having a grudge against the rest of the world, boyfriends, love-bites, staying out late, the usual. The problem was, my parents didn't have the time to handle it. With five kids to bring up, Mum just snapped and put me into care. It was drink and the arguments you see. The way I thought about my mother, I believed it was a good thing to happen and the first time in care, I enjoyed it.'

Louise stayed in state care for two months, made friends, and started to make progress. However, her mother took her back, saying she could cope. After a while the relationship turned sour and Louise was placed in care again. 'This time I didn't like it. Everybody was older and had been in care a lot longer than me, and I just couldn't relate to them at all. I'd say I didn't mind, but honestly, I didn't enjoy it. I was trapped, because I couldn't go home either. I was nowhere.'

After six months going to and fro between care and her parents and an auntie, Louise turned sixteen. Her parents threw her out of the house, once and for all. She subsequently moved into her boyfriend's flat for the next ten months, but this ended in tears. Louise eventually landed a place in a hostel in the centre of Cardiff, where the sudden painful experience of being homeless and alone became very apparent.

'I felt really lonely and that no one really cared, it was a feeling of rejection more than anything else. But I was really lucky, because I discovered the Cardiff Youth City Project, and met lots of people like me, all writing, painting, or doing something creative.'

It was at this time that Louise started writing poetry. 'It all started with a competition. At the time, a kid I knew tried to commit suicide. He was really small and loveable but a bit of a wally. I decided to write about the experience of talking him out of it·and of listening to his problems. The poem turned out to be very strong, and I completely surprised myself when I won the competition. To me, poetry is a form of justification for what I feel is right for me, and I just unlock it straight onto paper. Most of my thoughts and work are secret because hardly anybody of my age group can understand what I'm saying, so I don't bother.'

Louise says her most powerful pieces are 'Night' and 'Lust'. She explains,'I met this guy and we started to talk. Basically I wanted to use him for my fantasies, by turning the tables around and he knew it. We actually talked about it in the pub, what we would do in bed. I didn't feel he had used me and he certainly didn't mind either. It was just sex and lust, but not in a dirty way. What was a shock was that I didn't think it was going to actually happen. When the night of passion was over, the fantasy was over.'

Louise adds that what happened only happened once, but she is sure many girls and women think about the same thing without ever acting out their thoughts. If they do it is done with a lot of wishful thinking and secrecy.

Louise comments that the penalties for showing her affection are ignorance from her boyfriend and a confidence conflict on her part. 'It's reached a point of predictability so I know not to talk about my feelings and desires. I know I will get hurt if I do. I wish that I could though.

All I want is to be loved and men are scared of that. I can't understand why men can't say what they feel.

'After 'Night' and 'Lust', I never told a man what I really wanted and I struggled in silence because I didn't want to be rejected. Rejection is my enemy, you see, I hate it. My poetry is the only place where I can trek across my galaxy of fantasy secretly. I love it because no one can interfere or say it is wrong.'

In these recessionary times, Louise sends a very strong message that love and family are the powerbase of any country. 'I know some of it is my fault, but I wish I could have formed a relationship with my parents. I believe if you have any love then you should be honest and show it, otherwise you don't get anywhere. I don't think people understand what love is any more; it's just a hug, a kiss or talking. Writing poetry about my feelings helped me understand that, and made me realize my innocence, which maybe I still have in a way. I suppose I want to shut my eyes so I can't see any of the poverty around me or problems and just lose myself in words. I know when I eventually have my own kids, I will think of them as well as myself, so I can fix it before they go wrong.'

NIGHT

It begins at night. A drink down the pub,
I sit down by a man with bright blue eyes.
We start to talk and then I begin to flirt.
Undo his shirt with my eyes.
Feeling the hairs on his glistening chest.
Further down I venture till I handle the fruitful
parts of his loin, it's hot and moist, gleaming in
the candle-lit room.
Did I frown or blush?
No I became red hot with fiery passion, finally
I could hold out no longer, I made my move.
Down I went. I pat the firmness of his thigh
and back again, until finally he grabbed the
fruits of his labour, and oh, it was ecstatic. I
rose to uncontrollable excitement.
Oh my God, I cried.
Ooh I'm coming, I sighed.
He too totally agreed and confirmed this by
ejaculating sweet love juice inside me.
The best I've ever had.
Conclusion.
Again???

Louise Ambridge

LUST

Now I've had what I've been longing for.
Something's missing.
Was I in love or was it just a sexual fantasy.
Finally grasping what I thought I could never have.
There's nothing to hope for.
Now what?
Maybe it's someone else's turn to be in my fantasies.

Now I'm bored, I lusted for it, I finally got what I lusted
For...does he remember everything?
Moments of lust passed from his body to his.
We became one and then separated.
He lay there afterwards sleeping like an innocent baby.
I got up, dressed and left the fantasy that came true.

It's over.

Louise Ambridge

FEAR OF LOVE

Please don't hurt me more than you have to
Unwanted. Unloved.
Popular, but I feel alone.
Am I always second best,
Or am I number one?
You want me there but there's someone else.

Think about this situation.
Are you being hurt, who you are hurting.
I love you, yet fear the emotion I feel.
rejection is my enemy.
Lust is my weakness.
Is there wrong in that?

I lust for you. I want you near me.
What are you thinking?
Am I immature, young, too young for your
adult superiority?
If I could be sure of what you
are thinking
I'd make my move.

Louise Ambridge

METAMORPHOSIS

A new life,
a new age,
a new generation.
Hearing but not seeing, not knowing.
Learning day by day
new words, new things to do, new things to see.
Becoming aware, your senses awaken.
Growing, yearning for knowledge.
Intelligence, independence, adolescence.
Flee from the nest, leave the warmth.
Free from the chains, missing the warmth.
Cold, hungry but indefatigable.
Living life on the razor's edge.
Bonding, you marry.
Eggs of life appear. Grow, flee.

Old, thin.
Be true to yourself.
The body rots with age and so the mind grows wiser.
Reflection. Reflection of age, of weakness.
Delicate, fragile, yet strong as an ox.
Having battled life's ups and downs, pains and pleasures.
Mockery from all points.
Filling time.
Lonesome.
Digging your grave.
An extra nail in the coffin.
Another close shave.
Frightened, you give in.
Enter the windows of death.
Sourness, bitterness, mourning, death.

After death, re-incarnation.
After re-incarnation. re-occurrence, repetition.
Enter the window of life.
Is it all worth it?

Louise Ambridge

Canary Wharf offices, (over half remain empty), Isle of Dogs, London, 1993.

PMT

you're in a mood
they don't know why
you feel depressed
you start to cry
tired, aching
on your feet
dizzy, sick
you feel beat
carry on and on
everything's OK
the pain is strong
it won't go away
you're only a woman
people have said
but what do they know
you should be in bed
forget about the moods
forget about the pains
no one cares
it's that time of the month again.

Louise Ambridge

NIGHTMARE

You were there last night in my dreams,
hot sweaty, I woke in screams,
I was terrified of your touch,
but you didn't seem to notice much,
how hard you were hurting me.
I looked and I could see,
the devil in your face -
not that you seemed out of place,
corrupting my tender emotions.
Tearing my heart apart,
you know I'm not that sort.
So why did you touch the forbidden fruit,
why were your actions absolute.
You didn't even apologise.
You just looked at me with those creepy eyes
making me feel dirty, cheap,
each and every day of the week,
fifty-two weeks of the year,
while you snigger and sneer -
at me.

Louise Ambridge

SUICIDE

There's more to me than meets the eye
yes I look all smiles but inside I cry
for I've been hurt many times
but please don't listen to my whims or whines
for I'll get over these times of hate
I only hope it's not too late
to forget about the depressing things in life
before I use those razors or knives
to end my short and dreary existence
let's hope my friends are persistent
at trying to make me feel better today
instead of me wasting my valuable life away.

Louise Ambridge

'Paradise Found'. Sky, euphoric after successfully helping place a 'Section 6' order to legalise over a hundred homeless people to squat in empty office space, Soho, London, 1993.

Flowers commemorating the death of James Bulger, Liverpool, 1993.

Self-planned housing by residents, with council, Eldonian Village, Liverpool, 1993.

'Pops', Big Issue vendor, Embankment, London, 1993.

Anonymous poetry

Poems become anonymous for thousands of reasons, each one representing a part of someone's life. Poems that are written in pain or suffering are rarely produced for comment or to be seen, so anonymity is inherent in the act of writing. Words on paper are often a stream of torn consciousness, yet they can be hugely cathartic in effect, sometimes radically changing a person's outlook on life. The author rarely sees himself as a 'poet', just a communicator of a personal truth, in a moment of time.

A poem remains anonymous because someone has written it in an impossible place, both physically and mentally. A poem that will leave no trace of the writer is usually a cry for help and understanding: from a child suffering sexual abuse, a runaway freezing on the streets, a young prostitute caught up with a pimp, an addict trying to come off drugs, a mother stuck with her children in bed and breakfast, a prisoner wrapped up in the cycle of crime, or a person who has committed suicide and whose poem is their suicide note, left to a friend or a homeless day centre. Anonymity, therefore, is often absolute.

Some homeless poetry writers want their poems to be seen and their names known. In this book they form the majority. In the outside world these poets form the minority. *The Big Issue*'s writing groups and other creative writing centres which are forming throughout the country are touching an infinite wealth of poetry. The skill of these groups is that in developing a technical confidence they are enabling homeless people back into mainstream society. Being published in *The Big Issue* or other homeless magazines makes them visible. The anonymous poets in this book are a tribute to those who have had the strength, or opportunity, to come forward. For they were anonymous once too.

top left
  Rotherham Branch of care leavers (NAYPIC) lobbying Parliament for adequate after-care provision, 1993.
top right
  On March 31st 1993, government funding ended for Constable Wallard's 65-70 per cent successful Urban Crime scheme for deprived youths likely to (re-)offend, Liverpool, 1993.
bottom left
  The Big Issue writing group, London 1993.
bottom right
  Jobs rally, Hyde Park, London, 1993.

'Positive Graffiti,' 1993.

FOR NOTHING

Surround me in your love.
You are my walls.
Within these walls I
am safe.

Fill me with your spirit.
Make me feel your joy.
Help me
to grow in life.

You are my protector.
You do all this for nothing,
for I
am your son.

I DECREE

Joy in life,
to be in the warmth of innocence.
I have seen the pain.
I have tasted the poison.
No longer do I stand as one
with peace.
Maybe I know too much of the darkness
and I lay so far from the light.
Who can help me?
You.
I decree that, in my lonely world
You lie with me.

VICELANDS

Morals as shallow
to be nonexistent.
Something I must experience.
Vicelands.

Dark corners
hide men studying, watching.
A night of a thousand faces.

Cruisers eager to buy
young flesh for their distorted needs,
minds of young rent boys.

Sexual identity is ignored
in vicelands.

THE LABYRINTH

In the crazy labyrinth of time,
where memories plant seeds,
and dreams trace human needs,
I watched the patterns weaving
grotesque and shadowy forms.

It was a vast enigma, full of twisting circles
and weird crossing lines.
Then suddenly the vision cleared,
and I saw the labyrinth as merely
man's distorted vision of reality.

The arches were his man-made gods,
the crossing line his senses.
The word patterns
the war within himself.
The labyrinth his barbarity.

Yet from this gruesome imagery,
there suddenly appeared
the blinding light of reason.
And the blazing torch
of mankind's creativity.

Such as the vision of true reality,
that all wise men have seen,
which barbarians have ignored
as though it was obscene.

Today's barbarians
are still that way inclined.
That's why their reasoning is so deformed
and warfare plays mankind.

'Upside-down World', Nick Day after renovating his squat with his sculptures made from waste, Brixton, 1993.

UNTITLED

I put a finger into the water
Drew circles,
Watched the ripples spread
Minnows dart,
Tadpoles' tails waving to me
As I watched them depart.

How different then
Days of radiant innocence;
Hands cupping chin
As I lay in the long grass,
No urgency or animosity
And no visions of sadness.

Those beautiful blue skies
Expansive and timeless,
Fields full of buttercups
Daisies and bluebells
Enraptured I dreamt
Of elves and wishing-wells.

The faint rumble of distant thunder
Grew louder,
Puberty cracked the shell
Split the embryo
I fell upon those bleak black rocks
I never knew which way to go.

Those moments embroiled
Tangled upon that sparkling web
Bludgeoned and ill used
The light paled, an old ruin
Leapt from the mist
And there it stayed.

Disfigured, ungainly thing
Shambling along
Pulling stale food from a dustbin!

SO, HERE I AM AGAIN

So,
Here I am again,
Head swimming, heart caught
In a web of happiness
Spun out of time.

I hide
In the light of a thousand suns,
That radiate joy
Like a wind through the leaves
On the tree of life.

My mind floats,
Spinning in whirlpools
Of ecstasy.
Rivers of desire flood through me,
Bathing my soul
With a myriad of thoughts
And hopes for futures to come.

The rivers flow
Into the everlasting seas of life,
And my soul sails its course
On the eternal tides of truth,
Searching with questions
And with hope
For lost horizons yet to be formed,
And shores as yet untrod.

UNTITLED

From the top of a man-made precipice
Looking out on a world of phallic concrete,
We're still building Jacob's ladder,
Trying to reach heaven.

From the top of Nature's eminence,
Looking out on a world of green and gold.
We're still up there with the birds,
Still worshipping Icarus,
Trying not to fall to earth.

BORN TO BE FREE

Dolphins play in an open sea
Wild animals born to be free
You wonder at them in a cage
They do tricks in a circus ring
Remember they are a living thing!
Your love and care they must not miss
Why not swim with a dolphin
And give it a kiss?

March for jobs rally, Hyde Park, London, 1993.

HOMELESS

H is for HYPOCRISY you
see it every day

O is for the OBSTACLES I
wish they'd go away

M is for the MAZE I know
that is a trap

E is for the EXIT path I wish I
had a map

L is for the LONELINESS I
find myself entwined

E is for the ENCOURAGE
MENT I have within my mind

S is for SOLITUDE I know
in every way

S is for SORROW I carry
every day

That's how I spell HOMELESS,
that's what homeless means to
me.

WORDS

God made a world of loveliness
With trees and flowers and birds
But the most precious thing of all
He made
Were kind and gentle words.

"To see an idea being born into the world is a wonderful moment. From *A Sheltered Flame* is a direct political act from a spiritual conviction: that to survive in this world we must do more to help each other."

Martin Dunkerton, photographer, book co-ordinator, co-editor.

"A small voice in plea can't be heard, but many voices can. Working on the book has been an enlightening experience that I gained more from than I gave. I hope those that read the book feel the same experience and in turn can enlighten others."

Allan Meaken, co-writer.

"We are only aware of statements, of nothings, of presumed misunderstandings. Hopefully the book will clarify some of those misunderstandings."

Alison Traille, poet

"Life is thanks."

Tay Devlin, poet.

"People pass me by on the streets, not realising that only months ago I had everything: a girlfriend, home, job and car. After being made redundant I lost everything. People don't realise how quick it can be, The book's message is a positive one, and has given me a wonderful second chance."

John Gregg, assistant designer.

"What this country and in particular my generation lack is a common unity and cause. The positive approach of this book should move all of us one step closer to achieving those worldly ambitions and aims. I have learnt to adapt my individuality for the common love of mankind. I hope you do the same."

Sky, co-editor, writer, poet.

"I never thought the book would get off the ground. I'm so glad people had the faith to make it happen. It has shown me things I'm capable of, which I would never have realised before. Now I feel more confident that I can go out and really achieve."

Louise Ambridge, poet.

"I would like to say thank you to everyone for their patience in making this book, it's really important that people find out the truth about homelessness."

Sandra Clifford, poet, portrait photographer.

"Same grey, different day."

Alf Welton, poet.

"This book is an extension of myself, a sleeping giant awakened mysteriously, waiting for the hand of providence to close and show the world of my talent."

Ian Bryne, poet.

"My poems are now about a better world where people don't harm each other or our environment. They are about how we could all live together if we tried, without poverty or homelessness. Just peace."

Lizz Knight, poet.